# Human Capital AND Economic Development

Sisay Asefa
and
Wei-Chiao Huang
*Editors*

1994



W.E. UPJOHN INSTITUTE for Employment Research
Kalamazoo, Michigan

**Library of Congress Cataloging-in-Publication Data**

Human capital and economic development / Sisay Asefa and Wei-Chiao Huang, editors.
p. cm.
Includes bibliographical references and index.
ISBN 0–88099–148–8 — ISBN 0–88099–147–X (pbk.)
1. Human capital. 2. Human capital—United States. 3. Economic development. 4. United States—Economic conditions—1993–
I. Sisay Asefa, 1950– . II. Huang, Wei-Chiao.
HB501.5.H86 1994
338.973—dc20 94–22612
CIP


300 S. Westnedge Avenue
Kalamazoo, Michigan 49007–4686

The facts presented in this study and the observations and viewpoints expressed are the sole responsibility of the authors. They do not necessarily represent positions of the W. E. Upjohn Institute for Employment Research.

Cover design by J. R. Underhill
Index prepared by Shirley Kessel.
Printed in the United States of America.

# Preface

This book contains six essays, the first five of which are based on presentations made at the twenty-ninth Annual Public Lecture Series sponsored by the Department of Economics, Western Michigan University during the academic year 1992–93. The final essay is based on a public lecture delivered by a University Visiting Scholar in Economics during the fall of 1993.

In co-directing the public lectures and in preparing this book, we are first indebted to the authors of the essays without whom this volume would not have been possible. We are grateful to our colleagues in the Department of Economics at Western Michigan University for their support during our effort in organizing and directing the Lecture Series and the Visiting Scholar Program. We are thankful to the College of Arts and Sciences and the W. E. Upjohn Institute for Employment Research for their co-sponsorship of the Lecture Series, and we thank the University Visiting Scholar Program for sponsoring the public lecture on which the final essay of the volume is based.

We are also thankful to the members of the Economics Department Lectures Committee for the 1992–93 academic year, Professor Emily Hoffman of Western Michigan University, and Dr. Timothy Bartik of the W. E. Upjohn Institute for Employment Research.

Finally, we express our thanks and appreciation to the W.E. Upjohn Institute for Employment Research for their cooperation and the high quality of editorial services rendered in the publication of this volume.

Sisay Asefa and Wei-Chiao Huang
Kalamazoo, Michigan, January 1994

## CONTENTS

# Human Capital AND Economic Development

# Introduction

Sisay Asefa and Wei-Chiao Huang
*Western Michigan University*

Human capital, as viewed by economists, involves a process of investment that enhances human labor productivity by means of advances in knowledge and its applications. It specifically involves investment expenditures on education, training, health, nutrition, and related factors that increase the productivity of the labor force. Nobel Laureate T. W. Schultz (1956) was one of the first economists to identify the deficiency of the standard neoclassical production function in neglecting the critical role of human capital. More recent empirical studies of economic growth by Hagen (1980), Denison (1985), and Jorgenson (1988), have shown that human capital investment has made a significant contribution to the economic growth of industrial nations such as the United States. The essays in the present volume explore the various national and international dimensions of human capital and development ranging from the economic implications of demographic trends in the United States (Richard A. Easterlin), the effect of population growth and human capital on development (D. Gale Johnson and Julian L. Simon), the relationship among human capital, the family, and economic development (Mark R. Rosenzweig), and the crucial issue of workplace training in the United States (Peter B. Doeringer and Ann P. Bartel).

In the first essay, Easterlin begins by challenging Benjamin Wattenberg's book, *The Birth Dearth,* which predicts a decline of the United States economy due to an aging population and low fertility over the next century. Easterlin presents the rationale offered by Wattenberg and others for their pessimistic views about the economic effects of future demographic trends of the United States. He makes the argument that these popular views about the adverse effects of declining population growth on future economic development do not stand up to long-term historical facts. In supporting his thesis, he examines the historical record of selected Western industrial countries over the last century. These data include demographic variables such as the historical relationships between population growth and economic growth, the size of the total dependency burden (youth and old age) in relation to the rate of economic growth, the size and age of the labor force, and the implication for overall educational/human capital level of the labor supply. Based on these demographic data over the last century for eleven Western industrial nations including the United States, Easterlin concludes that the historical experience and evidence raise serious doubt about the "secular stagnation thesis." He notes that projected demographic trends are quite small by historical standards, and the projected aging of the labor force is within the range of historical experience. He further contends that any rise in old-age dependency will be offset by declining youth dependency for the United States and Western industrial nations, and that the projected total dependency rates are, on average, similar to the late nineteenth century for these countries, thereby casting some doubt on the whole stagnation thesis. The leveling of fertility below replacement level is not out of line with the data on completed fertility in this century, according to Easterlin. These data show long-term fluctuations of about half a century duration, and that the emerging labor market conditions seem to favor a new upswing; the data show a total fertility rate above the 1980 trough for all the countries examined. Easterlin points out that even the possibility of a new baby boom, dismissed by existing demographic projections, cannot totally be ruled out.

In the next essay, Johnson takes up another aspect of human capital—focusing on the value of a human being with little or no formal investment. His essay is relevant to low-income countries of the world with relatively low human capital investments of their populations. In examining the evidence on the effect of population growth on per capital income growth of developing countries, Johnson challenges the popular view of the negative relationship between population growth and per capita income in developing countries, as advanced by the proponents of "the Population Bomb Thesis." His essay summarizes some of the major findings of a working group organized by the National Research Council of the National Academy of Sciences, which is also critical of the pessimistic view about the effects of population growth on economic growth of developing countries. Johnson presents three empirical propositions that cast serious doubt on the commonly held view about the negative relationship between per capita income and population growth. First, significant increases in per capita income in Western industrial nations occurred between the eighteenth and twentieth century when their populations were also rising rapidly and life expectancy was increasing. Second, developing countries achieved higher per capita income, a rise in life expectancy, and reduced infant mortality since about 1950, when population growth began to rise rapidly. Specifically, Johnson points out the fact that between 1950 and 1980 developing countries experienced a rapid population growth of over 2 percent, paralleled with per capita income growth of 2.6 percent. Third, he presents evidence from regression results based on cross-country data that show no significant relationship between population growth and economic growth. According to Johnson, other variables such as economic policy, may be more important than population and human capital variables included in these results. He supplements this view by referring to recent empirical evidence by Levine and Renelt (1992) which presents results on the effect of various policy factors and population growth on the economic growth of 119 countries. None of the regressions showed a significant relationship between population and economic growth. Thus, Johnson makes the point that much of the human suffering in developing countries over the years has been caused by nonpopulation growth factors such as civil wars, state policy failure, and economic mismanagement. Johnson also summarizes some findings related to nine questions that came out of the NRC report on population growth and economic development that deal with the effect of population growth on the supply of exhaustible and renewable resources, environment, worker productivity, levels of schooling and health, income inequality, rural-urban migration, and social costs of fertility. He concludes that there is little evidence from this report "to support the position that a family imposes negative externalities on society when it chooses to have another child." He qualifies his argument, however, by pointing out that a very high population growth in excess of 3 percent in the short run, "may reduce rates of per capita income growth primarily due to the stress placed on institutions such as education, health, and city public services," and so NRC's evidence is more relevant to a moderate population growth rate of 1.25 to 2.5 percent. Governments of developing countries should, according to Johnson, pursue social and economic programs such as primary education, maternal and child health care, and social security programs that have the external effect of reducing population growth. He concludes his essay by presenting a rationale for what he calls "positive population policy," whose aim is to assist "every family in a country to have the number of children each family desires" without coercion. For such a policy to materialize, governments must provide relevant information, including contraceptive materials and services, to every household on a voluntary basis.

Rosenzweig's essay explores the relationship among human capital, the family, and economic development. He examines two related aspects of this complex relationship. First, whether family relationships and stability are related to the rate of economic growth. Second, how economic development affects the level and returns to investment on human capital. Realizing that the study of these relationships is a complex task in the context of a modern industrial economy such as the United States, he bases his analysis on data from the simpler (developing) economy of rural India. He uses time-series data that describe farm household behavior under traditional technology and cross-section data on farmers across India before and after the green revolution technical change. He organizes his essay by first discussing some key features of a traditional agrarian economy before technical change, including the relationship between family stability and human capital under this setting. After examining his data on the features of a traditional economy, he includes some evidence on specific hypotheses about the relationship between human capital and family structure with emphasis on risk-mitigation and experience as important elements of human capital. Rosenzweig then examines how technical change affects human capital investments and family structure, and draws some possible policy implications. According to Rosenzweig, experience (learning by doing) is the most valuable form of human capital under traditional static technology. Consequently, education which enables farmers to acquire knowledge outside such environment, provides little or no return. It follows that the elders have the largest amount of human capital and respect, resulting in family stability and intergenerational interdependence. The introduction of technical change, however, reduces the value of past experience and erodes family ties, which leads to family breakups and instability even though the rate of return from formal schooling may increase. Thus, according to Rosenzweig, technical change can have a destabilizing effect on the family by reducing returns from experience, by decreasing the role of risk-spreading arrangements among family members, and by weakening coping mechanisms in an uncertain traditional economic environment. Another important policy implication that he draws from these findings is that a significant decline in fertility in growth areas relative to other areas of India was achieved without any direct intervention by the government, indicating that such efforts are unnecessary in an environment of continuous technical change and economic growth.

In the following two essays, Doeringer and Bartel both deal with the issue of workplace training in the United States. Doeringer's essay is concerned with whether the workplace training system of the United States will survive international competition. He points out that the crux of the nation's human capital deficiency problem may not be due to its schools, and that educational reform may not be central to solving the problem, especially in the short run. Instead, he notes, the problem may be rooted in the weakening of the nation's workplace system for raising labor productivity, which he defines broadly to include effort, commitment, problem-solving capacity, and job skills. Doeringer's view is that while educational improvement may be an important part of a long-term solution, it is unlikely to rebuild the productive capacities of the present workers who are already out of school and who will constitute two-thirds of the labor force during the next decade.

Doeringer further examines some features and experiences with such alternative systems of workplace training in the United States as the Fordist system, the high-commitment system, and the low-wage, Employment-at-Will System. The traditional Fordist system involves raising productivity through "soft bargains" reached collectively between labor and management. The high-commitment system emphasizes individual rather than collective effort bargains to encourage the individual worker to internalize the goals and objectives of the company and to take action to achieve these goals. The employer in return provides intensive career training and development, fair compensation, and an implicit guarantee of permanent employment, with a result of continuous improvement in productivity and career earnings. The relatively new employment-at-will system allows firms to keep wages as low as market competition will allow, with an indefinite period of employment that quickly adjusts to changing labor market conditions, with no commitment from employers and no expectations of job security by workers. He observes that such firms do not invest on human capital development and do not depend on effort bargains, but rely on market incentives to motivate training investments and effort. Doeringer's essay is also concerned with the evolution of workplace training systems and their effects on productivity. His view is that it is an open question whether the traditional Fordist and high-performance workplace systems will survive in some form in the future labor market or if the low-wage, employment-at-will model will prevail.

Bartel analyzes another dimension of the issue of workplace training in the United States. Her essay is concerned with whether American workers are getting sufficient on-the-job training or if workplace training is underproduced. She explores this question by reviewing data available on the amount of training received by U.S. workers relative to other industrial countries, by examining data on the rate of return to investments in on-the-job training, by evaluating alternative suggestions to alleviate the underinvestment problem, and finally by discussing her own research findings about the relationship between technological change and training.

Bartel identifies two general sources of data, based on surveys of individual workers and employers, to study workplace training. She notes that both types of data report underinvestment. Even though the National Longitudinal Surveys of Mature Men, Young Men, Young Women, and Youth (NLSY) are the best employee-based sources of data, according to Bartel, these data have some measurement problems, as they do not measure informal training. Informal training appears to be quite important for U.S. workers, since it is found to occur at the same rate as formal training programs.

Bartel's essay also examines comparative training systems in three industrial countries: Germany, France, and Japan. The German system, which is based on an apprenticeship contract signed between a company and the government, is too rigid and narrow. Thus, it cannot be shown that German workers are better or more trained than American workers if the various dimensions of training are considered. The French system relies on a mandated training tax where employers of ten or more workers must spend a certain proportion of their labor cost on continuous education and training of employees or pay tax equal to the required amount minus the actual training expenditures. It cannot be concluded that American workers receive less training than French workers because, while the training incidence is higher in France, its length is much shorter. Finally, the Japanese training system applies only to large firms that employ only one-third of the workforce. The majority of the workforce is employed in small firms where employment is not guaranteed and very little training is done.

While the comparative data do not provide any conclusive evidence to confirm relative underinvestment, Bartel uses the rate of return data to reach "a conclusion that there is underinvestment in job training" in the United States. She then explores some possible causes of underinvestment, such as higher relative turnover rate, inability of the employer to evaluate the quality of applicants' general skills, minimum wage constraint, and inability of young workers to pay for their own training.

Bartel addresses the merit of alternative policy options to increase investment in training, including government-provided training, payroll-based national training tax imposed on employers, and subsidies and incentives for employees from the government. She notes that these options, especially the first two, are generally inadequate.

Finally, Bartel examines the issue of training in relation to technological change and concludes, based on her own research, that employee training will increase as a simple by-product of technological change during the next decade. In sum, her essay shows that while the high rates of return to training may be consistent with a possible underproduction of training in the United States, technological change will increase the incentives for investment in training, thereby requiring no external government interference with the market for labor training.

The final essay by Simon addresses the issue of the very-long-run effect of human capital on economic progress. Simon's essay is in the tradition of his provocative and often controversial views on the effect of population on economic development. The basic question addressed in his present essay deals with "the cause of so many of the world's population now being long-lived and endowed with much wealth and a high standard of living, with an even larger proportion likely to enjoy these benefits in the coming decades," compared to several centuries ago. In other words, he queries "why the rapid progress of the past two centuries did not begin centuries or millennia earlier. ...Was there something extraordinary about the human numbers or the level of technology in 1700 or so?" His answer is simply that today's technology is the sum of increments of knowledge in the past, and the additional knowledge was produced by people and therefore must have been influenced by human numbers. He adds that other possible factors such as culture, politics, and economic and social systems are also influenced by numbers. Thus, Simon's basic hypothesis is that the size of human population as measured by population density and number of people combined with the technology produced by them is the root cause of the speed of economic progress. It is his view that had population been frozen at the level of some 10,000 years ago, economic progress would not have reached the present state. His basic rationale is the obvious notion that if there were more people there would be more human capital to create knowledge that leads to economic growth. Simon's essay provides some evidence in support of what he terms "population-induced social change" by reviewing some sketchy time-series and cross-sectional data on the relationship between population and rate of economic growth and between population and natural resource availability, including some evidence on the relationship between population and structural factors that affect the rate of economic growth. Simon's basic premise is that higher density and larger population were, historically, *necessary* conditions for economic progress. Whether they were *sufficient* depends on the nature of particular societies, which have also been capable of retrogressing with population growth. While he supports the basic Malthusian proposition as relevant in the short-run subsistence economy under static technology, Simon's model refers to the very-long-run effects of population growth as the only exogenous variable, while other variables, such as institutions and technology, are all endogenously determined. This leads to one of his major points, that "no other element was as essential as the combination of knowledge and population numbers" in the very long run. Thus, Simon's proposition is that human economic progress is a function of population numbers, and all related social and economic dimensions are a function of population size and density in the very long run. He reinforces this view by reviewing some historical evidence about how more people bring about more ideas, more knowledge, expanded markets and cities, and higher productivity and income over the long run. He notes that even the spread of diseases has been positively influenced historically by population, as for example a more dense population reduced the "virulence of mass killers" such as malaria by practicing intensive cropping.

Finally, we are impressed with the quality and insights of the essays resulting from this lecture series. The individual authors present a complementary and well-integrated approach that challenges conventional wisdom and views about the various dimensions of human capital and economic development from the domestic and international perspectives. Our aim in this introduction was to highlight some of the critical issues discussed. We invite the reader to explore the details and the fuller context of the various aspects of the subject in the chapters that follow.

## References

Denison, E.F. 1985. *Trends in American Economic Growth.* Washington, DC: Brookings Institution.

Hagen, E.E. 1980. *The Economics of Development.* Homewood, IL: Irwin.

Jorgenson, D.W. 1988. "Productivity and Post-War U.S. Economic Growth," *Journal of Economic Perspectives* 2, 4 (Fall): 23–41.

Levine, Ross, and David Renelt. 1992. "A Sensitivity Analysis of Cross-Country Growth Regressions," *American Economic Review* 82, 4: 942–63.

Schultz, T.W. 1956. "Reflections on Agricultural Production, Output, and Supply," *Journal of Farm Economics* 38: 748–62.

# The Birth Dearth, Aging, and the Economy

## Where Have We Been and Where Are We Going?

Richard A. Easterlin
*University of Southern California*

In his recent volume, *The Birth Dearth*, Benjamin Wattenberg sees the American economy, fettered by low fertility and an aging population, as grinding to a virtual halt over the next century. Wattenberg writes for a popular audience in a self-styled "speculative and provocative" fashion. But his work forms the tip of a substantial iceberg of recent scholarly opinion offering similar and even wider-ranging arguments about the longer-term economic prospects of the United States and other advanced industrial economies. In a nutshell, recent low rates of childbearing, "the birth dearth," by causing low or negative population growth and population aging, are seen as exerting a serious drag on the economy. This happens because of slower growth of markets, decreased productivity growth, and an increased burden of dependency.

These arguments are typically long on speculation but short on facts, especially with regard to history. I propose here to offer a corrective. First, I recapitulate briefly the theoretical arguments and note some counterarguments that have been advanced. Then I turn to the historical facts and assess the arguments in the light of actual experience, both that of the United States and of advanced western and northern European countries. If population growth plays such an important role in determining economic growth, then one would expect to find that population growth and economic growth go together. Is this, in fact, the case? And how do prospective rates of population growth compare with past experience—are they, for example, far lower than what has gone before? What of the outlook for the dependency burden? Does this involve magnitudes that appear unprecedented? How has economic growth varied with the dependency burden in the past? How serious is the prospective aging of the *labor supply*, as distinct from population? What are the implications of aging for the educational attainment of the labor supply?

In discussing these questions, I take as given (as do Wattenberg and others) the current projections of population stagnation here and abroad. Typically these projections come in three variants—high, middle, and low—with the middle projection being most favored. But even the high-fertility projection assumes only a modest eventual increase in rates of childbearing, to an average of around 2.1 births per woman. This magnitude of 2.1 is called replacement-level fertility, because it is the rate of childbearing per woman needed to maintain population size constant over the long run.

These projections—whether low, middle, or high—of future low fertility are critical to the forecasts of stagnating population and rising old-age dependency. But how much confidence can we place in projections that seek to peer a half century or more into the future? Does the history of population forecasting, and particularly of projections of rates of childbearing, argue for accepting these forecasts? If not, would alternative forecasts substantially alter the outlook for population aging? In the concluding section, I address these questions—in short, the prospective continuation of the "birth dearth" itself.

## Effects of Population on the Economy: Theoretical Arguments

The theoretical arguments are of two general types—one relating to the impact of population change on the demand for goods, the other relating to the impact on the supply or production capabilities of the economy (for specific references, see Easterlin 1991).

The demand argument focuses on the effect of a declining rate of population growth. The growth rate of population, it is said, governs the growth rate of markets, and thus of the demand for consumer goods and also capital goods such as housing, factories, and machinery. Declining population growth discourages business, causing markets to expand less rapidly or cease to grow altogether.

The arguments about supply-side effects stress the impact of population aging. The population is seen as comprising three parts—young, middle-aged, and older—with the older segment growing relative to the other two. Now assume that for any given attribute affecting production capabilities, say, physical strength, the older group is relatively low. Other things being constant, if the elderly's share of the population grows, then the average degree of physical strength in the population as a whole will decline. Aging of the population would thus reduce production capacity by lowering the physical capacity of the population.

The specific attributes to which this argument is applied are numerous. The older population is supposed to be less well educated, and thus less skilled. The older population is assumed to be less likely to save and thereby to finance capital accumulation. The older population is said to be more fixed in its ways, less innovative and creative, and thus an obstacle to technological progress. The older population is claimed to be less geographically and occupationally mobile, and therefore less able to take advantage of new opportunities essential to economic progress. In combination, these arguments assert that, in general, aging of the population will retard the growth of production capabilities by lowering the quality of the labor supply, reducing the rate of capital accumulation, and lessening the rate of technical progress.

In addition, the older population is said to be different in the type of dependency burden it presents. Per capita public expenditures on retirement and health are greater for the older population. Hence, as the proportion of elderly grows, so too will the proportion of taxes to income needed to finance public retirement and health spending. Thus the "burden of old-age dependency" raises the specter of an insupportable tax burden on the working-age population, lowering the motivation of workers to work and save.

Although this is a formidable set of arguments, it has not gone without challenge. Regarding the demand argument, it is pointed out that markets depend on total spending, not number of spenders. Even with the number of spenders constant, spending per person and thus total spending will continue to rise as per capita income grows. On the supply side, it is pointed out that arguments about physical strength are of dubious relevance to a labor force dominated by white-collar and service workers. Whether older workers are less educated depends on the historical nature of educational progress. Moreover, age stands for experience, and an older labor force is a more experienced labor force. Nor is it clear that the older population saves less; older persons, it is said, may be hesitant to spend down their assets because of uncertainty about health costs and the timing of death, as well as the desire to leave an inheritance.

As always, such "on the one hand," "on the other" arguments leave one in a sea of uncertainty. Hence the need for historical facts, to which we now turn.

## The Evidence

As we examine the facts, we look at the United States and at ten European nations in the forefront of the demographic changes that have caused concern. The population projections used are the same as those underlying the present gloomy forecasts of long-term economic stagnation.

### *What Has Been the Historical Relation Between Population Growth and Economic Growth?*

If population growth were a major factor influencing economic growth, then one might expect to find that higher population growth and higher economic growth go together. Is this, in fact, the case?

Figure 1 presents growth rates since 1870 of population and real per capita income for each of the eleven countries. Average growth rates over four long periods are given. The periods are those identified by Angus Maddison in his book, *Phases of Capitalist Development* (1982), as development "phases" common to these countries, except that the most recent period in his study, 1973–1979, has been updated to cover 1973–1986.

Studying the figure, one notes that fluctuations in the two series go together in most countries. Conceivably, one might seize on this to argue that declines in population growth cause declines in per capita income growth, but this is to argue that the tail wags the dog. Note that

**Figure 1. Rate of Growth of GDP Per Capita (solid line) and Population (dotted line), Specificed Country and Period 1870–1986 (percent per year)**

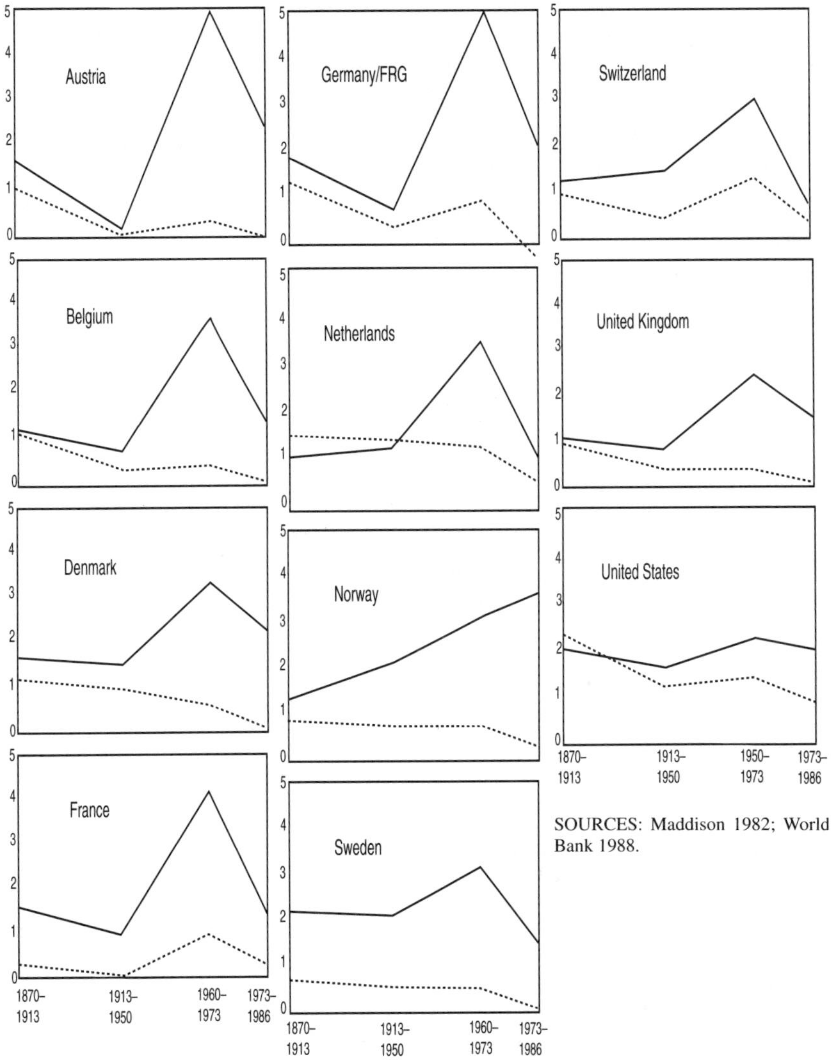


SOURCES: Maddison 1982; World Bank 1988.

in all countries the swings in population growth rates are quite small compared with those in per capita income growth.

Even more doubt about the importance of population growth in determining economic growth arises when one compares long-term *trends* in the two series. While population growth has trended downward in most of these countries over the last century, real per capita income growth has trended upward. Typically the two post-1950 observations on real GDP per capita in figure 1, including even that for the recent relatively depressed period, 1973–1986, lie above those for the two earlier periods. In contrast, the post-1950 rates of population growth are about the same as or lower than the pre-1950 rates. This inverse association between trends in economic growth and population growth is contrary to what one would have expected if declining population growth were exerting a serious drag on the economy.

### *How Sizable are Projected Declines in Population Growth Compared With Past Experience?*

The population growth rates projected for these countries in the next century are, in fact, not a great deal different from their current rates. The average annual growth rate of population in 1973–1986 was only 0.3 percent; the projected growth rate, at its lowest for the period 2030–2050 averages -0.3 percent (United Nations 1988b). The prospective decline in population growth rates is thus, on average, 0.6 percentage points over an interval of six decades, or a tenth of a percentage point per decade. As we have just seen, per capita income growth has trended upward in these countries, while population growth has trended downward. It is hard to believe that such a modest further decline in the rate of population growth would in itself produce a dramatic adverse departure from the historic pattern of secularly rising per capita income growth.

### *How Sizable Are Projected Increases in the Overall Dependency Burden Compared With Past Experience?*

The dependency burden is sometimes discussed as though it comprises elderly dependents alone, but it is obvious that the burden of dependency on the working-age population involves infants and children as well as older dependents. Thus, to put dependency changes in proper perspective, one needs to look at the size of the entire dependent population, young and old, relative to the working age population. To this end, figure 2 presents, for the same eleven countries since 1880, the ratio to the working age population aged 15–64 of the sum of the two dependent age groups, persons under age 15 and over age 64. Subsequently, we will consider the two age groups separately. The vertical broken line in each panel is at 1990, separating actual experience from projected. The horizontal line in each panel, about which most of the curves fluctuate, is at a value of 0.6, indicating that, on average in this period, there were about 0.6 dependents per member of the working-age population.

How sizable is the prospective increase in dependency when viewed in historical perspective? Figure 2 shows a projected peak in dependency for all of the countries in 2040, half a century hence. How does the height of this peak compare with the highest level reached in the past century? In three countries (France, Germany, and Switzerland) the projected peak is clearly higher; in three others (Norway, the United Kingdom, and the United States), clearly lower; and in the rest, it is about the same. On average, the total dependency rate in these advanced industrial countries will about match its historic high in the period since 1880. The projected levels in 2040 are clearly higher than those prevailing at the current time, and it is this contrast that gives rise to much of the current concern. But extending the period of comparison backward a full century, one finds that in only three of the countries is projected dependency higher than in the past. Moreover, in no case does the projected high fall outside of the past century's experience of these countries taken as a whole—the highest projected ratios are somewhat less than 0.8, as was true of the highest ratios in the late nineteenth century.

Thus, the outlook for the total dependency burden, when viewed against the experience of the past century, is not unprecedented. This conclusion holds under a variety of sensitivity tests. Varying the concept of dependency—for example, instead of population ratios, using nonworkers to workers—does not alter the picture. Nor does focusing on the "highly" dependent population, that is, old-old plus young-young. Neither do changes in the source used for the projections—OECD, UN, IMF, etc. Nor does allowance for wide variation in immi-

**Figure 2. Total Dependency Ratio, Actual and Projected, Specified Country, 1880–2050 (ratio of persons aged 0–14 and 65+ to those aged 15–64)**

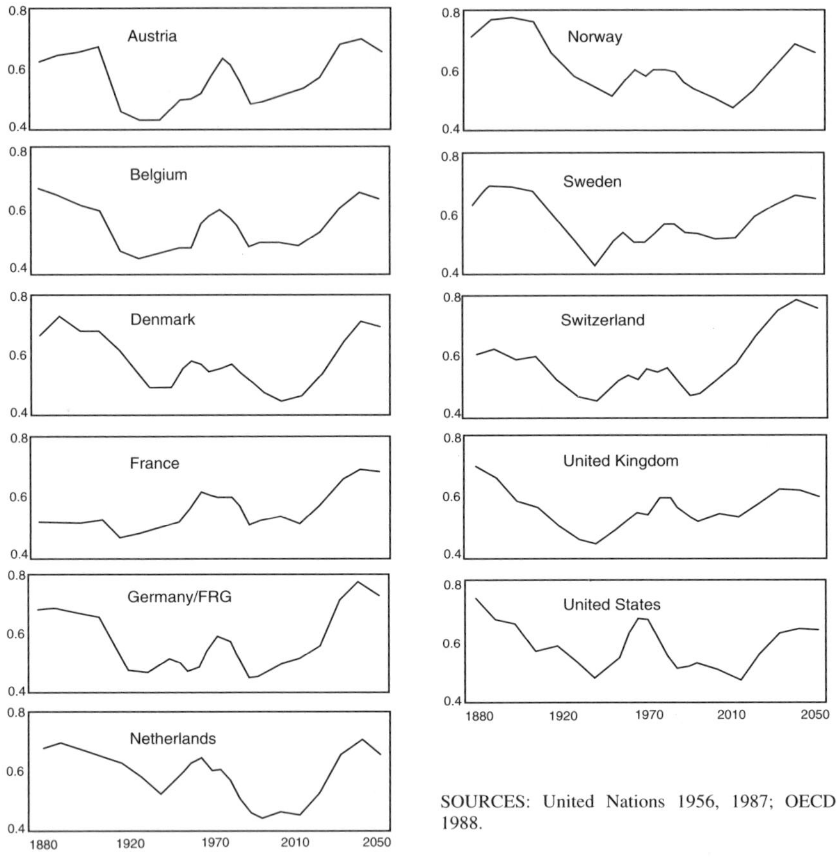


SOURCES: United Nations 1956, 1987; OECD 1988.

gration. Among current projections, the only case in which total dependency would rise to levels unprecedented in the past century is that which assumes a mortality revolution at the oldest ages. Although this possibility cannot be wholly ruled out, it is not this projection that underlies current gloomy accounts of the economic impact of population aging. Rather, such accounts are based on the more moderate mortality projections on which the projections used in figure 2 are based.

### *What Has Been the Historical Relation Between the Dependency Burden and the Rate of Economic Growth?*

Figure 3 bears on the relation between the dependency burden and the rate of economic growth. It is designed to assess whether increases in the dependency rate have been associated with decreases in the rate of economic growth. The four time periods used in figure 1 are again used here, 1870–1913 through 1973–1986.

As can be seen, although growth of total output (GDP) per capita (the solid line) has varied markedly from one period of economic growth to another, the total dependency rate (the dotted line) has not. In most of the countries, the dependency rate is highest in the period 1870–1913, thereafter it is fairly stable (figure 3). In the post-World War II period the contrast is dramatic. Growth rates of real per capita income in the period 1950–1973 were almost double those from 1973 to 1986, averaging 3.5 versus 1.9 percent. In contrast, in almost all of the countries, the dependency rate was nearly the same in the two periods, and the eleven-country average was, in fact, virtually identical, .55 versus .54. One would be hard put to argue that dependency had much to do with the dramatic post-1973 drop in economic growth rates, and not surprisingly, it is never mentioned in scholarly attempts to explain this decline.

### *What Does the Prospective Rise in Old-Age Dependency Imply for the Tax Burden on the Working-Age Population?*

Although overall dependency will not be so much different, the prospective age composition of dependency will be. As shown in figure 4, youth dependency is trending downward and old-age dependency upward. Seen in conjunction with the total dependency trend, this shift

**Figure 3. Rate of Growth of GDP Per Capita (solid line, right scale) and Average Total Dependency Ratio (dotted line, left scale), Specified Country and Period, 1870–1986**

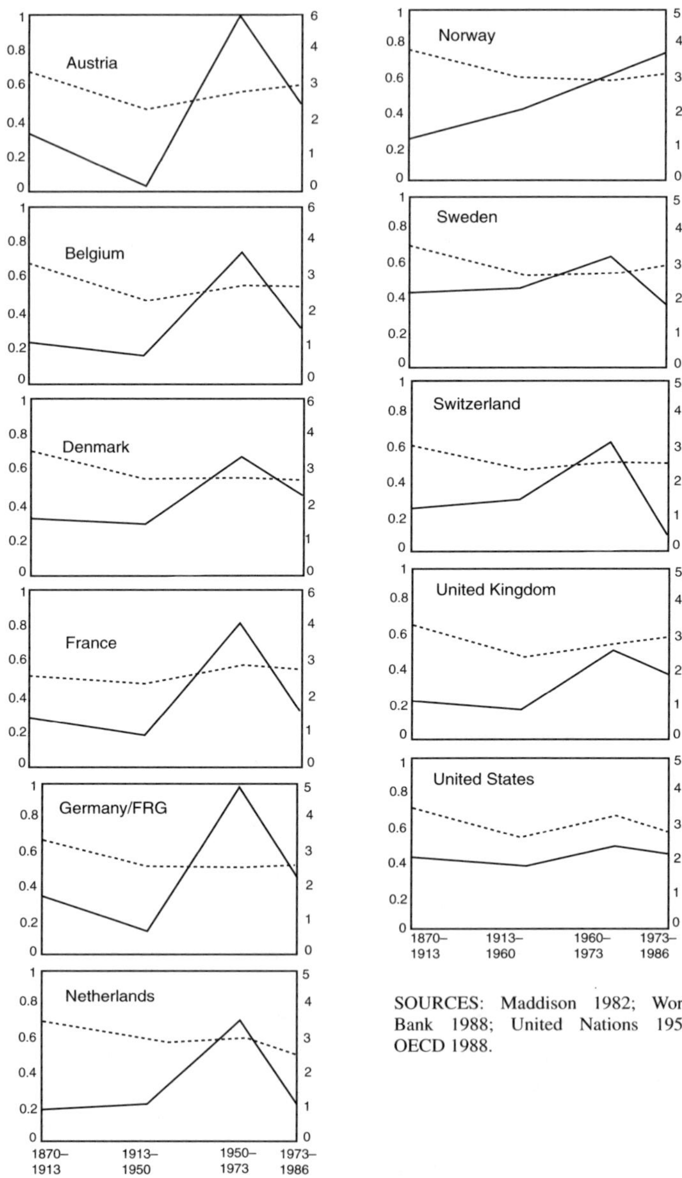


SOURCES: Maddison 1982; World Bank 1988; United Nations 1956; OECD 1988.

**Figure 4. Youth and Elderly Dependency Ratio, Specified Country, 1880–2020 (solid line = ratio 65+ to 15–64, broken line = ratio 0–14 to 15–64)**

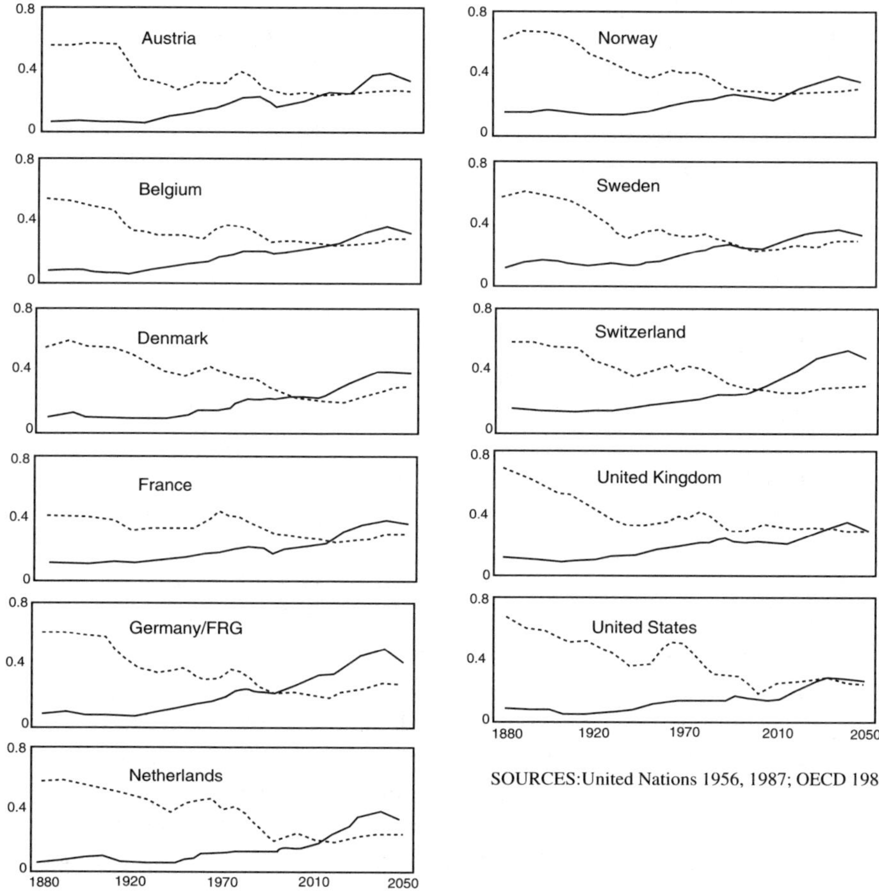


SOURCES: United Nations 1956, 1987; OECD 1988.

puts in a rather different light the issue of the prospective burden on the working population of rising old-age dependency. Clearly, a declining burden of young dependents compensates for a growing burden of older dependents. Analysts of government spending sometimes recognize this by noting the offset to rising government retirement and health spending provided by declining education expenditures (Holzmann 1988; OECD 1988). But the relevant comparison must go beyond this to consider the full economic costs per dependent, that is, the private as well as public costs of supporting infants and children compared with the elderly. If the working-age population needs to spend less out of its income to support children, then more funds are potentially available for supporting older dependents (United Nations 1988a).

It is one thing to count heads and compare the number of younger versus older dependents. It is another to assess the full economic costs of supporting an average younger versus older dependent. Clearly, the standard of support for both children and older dependents is socially, not physiologically, determined. Moreover, there is the need to consider nonmarket production and consumption of the two groups. Indeed, it is because of the ambiguity regarding costs of dependents that it is important to have a clear picture of the numbers of younger versus older dependents, as in figure 4.

The amount of empirical work that has actually been done on relative costs of the two groups is small, but what has been done suggests that economic costs per dependent (private plus public) are, in fact, not much different for older and younger dependents (Easterlin 1991). If this is so, then the economic burden of dependency on the working-age population is unlikely to be noticeably higher in the first half of the twenty-first century than in the twentieth century, since the increased cost of supporting a larger proportion of older dependents will be offset by the decreased cost of supporting a smaller proportion of younger dependents. This implies that the real issue to be faced is largely political, namely, how to capture via taxation the savings of households from supporting fewer younger dependents, so that these funds can be used to meet the rise in public expenditures needed to support older dependents. The question of political feasibility is a serious one, but it does not seem insurmountable, given that the workers to be taxed would themselves eventually be beneficiaries of such taxation. In any event, the issue is clearly different from that suggested by the view that the prospective *economic* burden on workers of support of dependents will somehow be unprecedented. This does not seem to be the case.

But what about the implications for the prospective tax burden on the working-age population? Clearly, if public expenditures grow relative to GNP over the long run, so too will taxes. For one thing, as was noted, increased public spending on retirement and health care would be partly offset by decreased public spending for schooling. Hence, the net increase in public spending and thus in taxes would be less than the increase in retirement and health spending. Moreover, as shown in table 1, projections to 2040 by OECD for most of the countries covered here, using the present demographic scenario, indicate that a quite modest average annual growth rate of real earnings (between 0.3 to 0.8 percent) would suffice to keep the tax burden per head of the working-age population in 2040 at the same level as in 1980. This growth rate of earnings is well below that experienced in the past. This projection assumes no change in benefit levels for the older population, but it also fails to allow for the fact that the taxable capacity of the working-age population would be enhanced by fewer younger dependents per worker and by higher labor force participation of females. Nor is there any allowance for a possible "peace dividend" due to the end of the cold war. Thus, it seems unlikely that there would be adverse incentive effects because of an undue tax burden associated with population aging.

### *How Sizable is the Prospective Aging of the Labor Supply, and What Does It Imply for the Overall Educational Level of the Labor Supply?*

What is the outlook for the age composition of the working-age population itself? Will there be, as some have argued, a disproportionate number of older workers and a consequent possible decline in innovation, mobility, and thus productivity growth? To assess this question, figure 5 presents data from 1880 through 2025 for the ratio of the population aged 20–34 to that aged 35–64, that is, the younger working-age population relative to the older. The trend in this ratio is clearly downward; there will be relatively fewer younger and more older workers. In most countries, however, the projected level around 2025 is not much below that around 1960. World Bank projections (Bulatao et al. 1990), which have ratios for 2025 much like those shown here, imply an increase to 2050 in the proportion of the *young* in all of the countries, ranging from 2 to 10 percentage points, as lower birth rate cohorts replace higher birth rate cohorts at ages 35–64. Thus, while a relative scarcity of younger workers (or surplus of older workers) is in prospect for the first quarter of the next century, it is not greatly out of line with the degree of scarcity experienced three decades ago, and it is projected to lessen between 2025 and 2050.

**Table 1. Average Annual Growth Rate of Real Earnings Per Worker Required to Maintain Tax Burden Per Worker Constant, 1980–2040, and Actual Growth Rate of Earnings, Eight Countries, 1965–1987 (percent per year)**

| Country | (1) Required growth rate, 1980–2040 | (2) Actual growth rate, 1965–1987 |
|---|---|---|
| Belgium | 0.3 | 4.1[a] |
| Denmark | 0.4 | 2.2 |
| France | 0.5 | 3.1 |
| Germany (FRG) | 0.7 | 2.9 |
| Netherlands | 0.6 | 2.9[a] |
| Sweden | 0.3 | 2.1 |
| United Kingdom | 0.2 | 2.4 |
| United States | 0.5 | 1.3[b] |

SOURCES: Column 1: Calculated from OECD (1988, p. 41). The OECD projection is based on the demographic projections underlying figure 2 and an assumption of constant age-sex specific labor force participation rates. Column 2: Compensation per employee in the business sector as reported in OECD (1990), adjusted by the consumer price index (OECD, various dates). The period used for the actual growth rates is the longest for which historical OECD data are available; United States data are since 1948.

a. 1970–1987.

b. 1948–1987.

What about the impact of labor supply aging on the educational attainment of the labor force? In considering this, one should note that in a number of these countries, the educational level of the older working-age population will improve substantially over the next thirty years, as those who benefited from the pre-1970s upsurge of schooling

**Figure 5. Ratio of Persons Aged 20–34 to 35–64, Actual and Projected, Specified Country, 1880–2025**

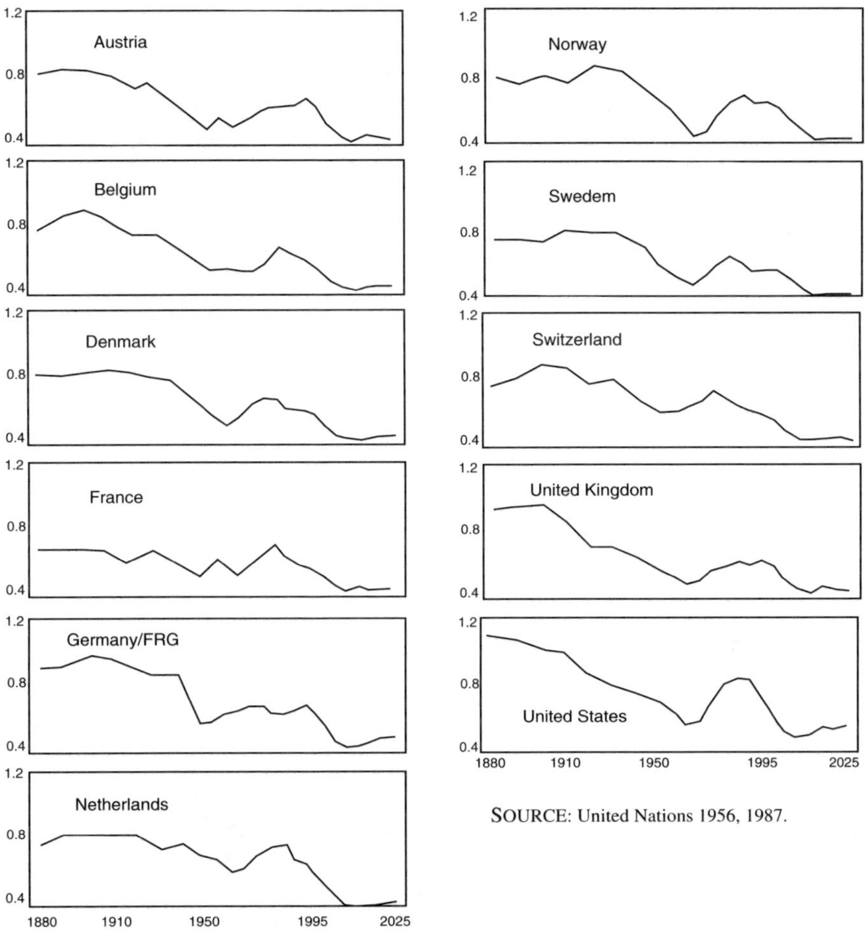


SOURCE: United Nations 1956, 1987.

reach older ages. Table 2 shows the prospective changes in educational attainment of older workers implied by recent census data. If schooling of the young continues to stagnate as it did in the 1970s (OECD 1983, 1984), the average level of education of the labor force as a whole would, nonetheless, be higher, as less-educated older cohorts are replaced by better-educated ones. If schooling of the young resumes its prior uptrend, then the average education of the labor force will rise even more. In either event, the favorable trend in educational attainment at older ages will offset the supposed adverse effect of aging on education of the labor supply.

**Table 2. Actual and Projected Percentage of Those Aged 55–64 Completing Secondary Level Education or Higher, Specified Country**

| Country[a] | Actual, c. 1970–1980 | Projected, 2000–2010 |
|---|---|---|
| Belgium | 21 | 53 |
| Denmark | 42 | 58 |
| France | 13 | 28 |
| Germany (FRG) | 21 | 28 |
| Norway | 37 | 63 |
| Sweden | 25 | 46 |
| United States | 57 | 84 |

SOURCES: United Nations (1974, 1980); U.S. Bureau of the Census (1984, 1987).

a. The age group for Denmark and Norway is 45–64; for Sweden, 55 and over. For Sweden, the percentage is for those with some secondary level education or higher.

There is a tendency to think of the older population in terms of the low educational levels that prevailed in the past. It is time to recognize that in many countries older workers will be much better educated than heretofore, and not much different in educational level from younger workers. In the future the generally higher educational level of older workers (and possible younger workers as well) should be an important factor, along with the greater experience of older workers, compensating for a negative effect, if any, of aging on innovation and mobility.

## The Outlook for the Birth Dearth

So far the analysis has accepted without question the view embodied in current population projections that fertility will remain quite low, perhaps declining further or rising to near-replacement levels at most. But how good are these projections? To answer this, one might reasonably ask: did population forecasters foresee either the enormous post-World War II baby boom or subsequent baby bust? The answer is no. While the baby boom was taking off in the late 1940s, population forecasters were still predicting a continuation of the low fertility rates of the 1930s. Eventually, in the 1950s, with the baby boom at full throttle, forecasters abandoned their low fertility projections for high fertility forecasts only to be caught by surprise once again as fertility started to plunge in the 1960s. In the last two decades, as fertility rates plummeted to new lows in advanced industrial countries, forecasters have switched back to low fertility assumptions, as in the forecasts we have just been examining.

How much faith can we put in the current projections? Not much. Rather than predicting the future, fertility projections basically track the recent past. Instead of admitting this, however, forecasters typically try to buttress their projections with supporting judgments. The latest United States Census Bureau *high* fertility projection foresees an eventual rate of childbearing only slightly above replacement, about 2.2 births per woman. In commenting on this, the Bureau assures us: "it is clearly possible that fertility might eventually surpass [this level]...but that does not seem likely given the social, economic, and demographic trends of the last two decades" (U.S. Bureau of the Census 1989, p. 21). Similarly, in a recent volume, authoritatively entitled *Future Demographic Trends in Europe and North America,* the United Nations' 1988 *high* projection of the total fertility rate (which also reaches an eventual mean value of about 2.2 for industrialized countries) is dismissed as "too high and not very probable." Instead, the author opts for fertility rates considerably below replacement levels as more probable, an average of about 1.6 to 1.9 births per woman (Klinger 1991, p. 159).

Such statements have a familiar ring. Over four decades ago, in 1948, the then leading American scholarly demographic publication opined regarding future fertility rates that "...the range of uncertainty is between rates somewhat below replacement and rates slightly above such replacement" (*Population Index* 1948). Needless to say, this statement was made *after* the post-World War II American baby boom was underway, when fertility soared far above replacement levels.

A similar fate may be in store for the more recent statements quoted above. As shown in table 3, in a number of advanced industrial economies, the total fertility rate in 1990 was noticeably above its 1980s trough, and in none was it below. The U.S. Census Bureau's *high* projection of total births in 1990, published in *1989*, was over 5 percent *below* actual experience. Even allowing for the fact that work on the projection was completed in 1987, how could the *high* projection fall so far short in only three years? Indeed, although the latest recession has put the usual damper on fertility, total births in 1991 were again above the high projection of the Census Bureau, by almost 4 percent. Compared with the medium projection, that used in the forecasts here, births in 1990 and 1991 averaged almost 12 percent higher than projected.

**Table 3. Current Total Fertility Rate (TFR) Compared With That at Most Recent "Baby Bust" Trough, Twelve Countries, 1980–Present**

| | Baby bust trough | | Current (preliminary) | | Percent change in |
|---|---|---|---|---|---|
| Country | Year | TFR | Year | TFR | TFR |
| Austria | 1987 | 1.43 | 1990 | 1.46 | 2.1 |
| Belgium | 1985 | 1.50 | 1990 | 1.62 | 8.0 |
| Canada | 1987 | 1.66 | 1990 | 1.76 | 6.2 |
| Denmark | 1983 | 1.38 | 1990 | 1.67 | 21.0 |
| France | 1983 | 1.79 | 1990 | 1.80 | 0.6 |
| Germany (FRG) | 1985 | 1.28 | 1990 | 1.48 | 15.6 |
| Netherlands | 1983 | 1.47 | 1990 | 1.62 | 10.2 |
| Norway | 1983 | 1.66 | 1989 | 1.88 | 13.3 |
| Sweden | 1983 | 1.61 | 1990 | 2.14 | 32.9 |
| Switzerland | 1985 | 1.51 | 1989 | 1.56 | 3.3 |
| United Kingdom | 1983-4 | 1.77 | 1990 | 1.85 | 4.5 |
| United States | 1986 | 1.77 | 1990 | 2.09 | 18.1 |

SOURCES: Calot (1988); Van de Kaa (1988); Monnier (1990); Monnier and Guibert-Lantoine (1991, p. 955).

Clearly, the fertility experience of the past few years here and abroad hints at the possibility of a new fertility upswing. Historical experience does provide a basis for projecting an upturn in fertility. If we extend our historical perspective beyond the past two decades, we find that over the past century there has been a long-term swing in fertility rates in almost all advanced industrial countries. This is illustrated by estimates of completed fertility presented in table 4. Typically, the initial trough occurs among women born near the beginning of the century and the subsequent peak among those born in the early 1930s. Although completed fertility for most women born in the two decades after World War II is not yet exactly known, the projected figures for women born in 1950, who are now very close to the end of their childbearing, are very similar to those of the cohorts born at the beginning of the century. A new upswing would extend this pattern nicely. Although the historical record does not prove that fertility will increase as in the past, recent experience hints at this. Certainly, the historical record suggests that an increase in fertility is a possibility that forecasters ought at least to recognize.

This possibility finds further support when we consider the prospective labor market for young adults in the coming decade. The numbers of those who will be reaching the childbearing ages will be unusually low, an echo of the recent baby bust. Also, immigration from low-income countries in Europe is likely to be increasingly restricted. Other things constant, this scarcity of younger workers will make for a favorable labor market for adults in the family formation ages, a reversal of the situation experienced by their predecessors, the baby boom cohorts. The biggest conjectural factor is the growth rate of aggregate demand. The prospective reduction in military outlays and consequent easing of spending pressures on government budgets give some basis for thinking there may be a return to the expansive monetary-fiscal policies of the earlier post-World War II era. Moreover, smaller numbers at the younger end of the labor market should make for more vigorous expansion of aggregate demand by the monetary-fiscal authorities by lowering the unemployment rate corresponding to full employment. If aggregate demand is expanded more rapidly, then demand-side conditions will also take a turn more favorable to young adults. Although the outlook is uncertain, it hardly warrants dismissing the possibility of a strong labor market for young people that would induce a fertility upswing.

**Table 4. Swings in Completed Fertility Since Around 1990**

| | Initial trough | | Peak | | Projected | |
|---|---|---|---|---|---|---|
| Country | Birth cohort (1) | Children per woman (2) | Birth cohort (3) | Children per woman (4) | Birth cohort (5) | Children per woman (6) |
| Austria | n.a. | n.a. | 1934 | 2.45 | 1950 | 1.90 |
| Belgium | 1905 | 2.01 | 1931 | 2.29 | 1950 | 1.80 |
| Canada | 1911 | 2.70 | 1930 | 3.39 | 1950 | 1.94 |
| Denmark | 1904 | 2.15 | 1933 | 2.39 | 1950 | 1.90 |
| England & Wales | 1906 | 1.81 | 1934 | 2.42 | 1950 | 2.00 |
| France | 1896 | 1.98 | 1930 | 2.64 | 1950 | 2.10 |
| Germany (FRG) | 1901 | 2.08 | 1933 | 2.32 | 1950 | 1.70 |
| Norway | 1906 | 2.01 | 1933 | 2.58 | 1950 | 2.10 |
| Sweden | 1905 | 1.81 | 1934 | 2.16 | 1950 | 2.00 |
| Switzerland | 1907 | 1.97 | 1933 | 2.20 | 1950 | 1.80 |
| United States | 1908 | 2.27 | 1933 | 3.24 | 1950 | 2.05 |

SOURCE: Calot (1988). The Netherlands is omitted because it does not have a swing in fertility. Compared with the other countries here, it starts at a much higher initial level (around 3 children per woman) and trends downward.
n.a.=not available.

Ongoing rates of childbearing, historical fertility experience, and the prospective labor demand-supply conditions for young adults thus suggest as a serious possibility a prospective upswing in fertility. If this possibility were introduced into projections it would, of course, substantially alter the outlook for population growth and dependency rates. Over the next decade or two, population growth and dependency would be higher than now projected as the population under 18 grew more rapidly than expected. (No doubt, there would also be a renewed upsurge of fears about excessive population growth.) But in the period when dependency is currently expected to reach projected highs, after 2025, there would be a tendency for the dependency ratio to decline as the newest baby boom cohorts reached adulthood and expanded the numbers in working ages.

While all of this is conjectural, it is hardly any more so than the prevailing consensus of a continued birth dearth. This consensus rests solely on a projection six decades hence of experience merely of the last two decades. It is hard to see why projections sixty years down the road should not be based on historical experience of at least comparable length. The possibility of a substantial fertility upswing would seem to deserve more weight in assessments of population prospects than is given to it currently.

## Summary

The central question at issue here is whether the demographic patterns projected for the future—low or negative population growth and population aging—are likely to have important adverse effects on future economic growth, that is, whether the projected patterns of population growth imply secular stagnation on the economic side. To answer this, we have focused particularly on the record of the last century.

As it turns out, historical experience raises serious doubt about this secular stagnation thesis. In the past, growth rates of real per capita income have trended upward despite a downward trend in population growth. This is hardly what one would expect if population growth were exerting a serious drag on the economy. Also, in the post-World War II period, economic growth rates have differed sharply between periods with little or no differences in dependency. Nor are projected demographic changes markedly out of line with past experience. Future declines projected for the rate of population growth are quite small; hence it is hard to see why a substantial new negative effect on economic growth should emerge. Projections of aging of the labor force itself do not yield magnitudes out of line with previous experience. Moreover, there will be a sharp increase in the educational attainment of older workers. Negative effects, if any, of labor force aging on innovation and mobility are likely to be offset by a markedly higher educational level of the older population, as well as the greater experience of older workers.

Similarly, the outlook for the total dependency burden on workers, when viewed in historical perspective, is not unprecedented. Projected total dependency rates are, on average, about the same as in the late nineteenth century, since rising old-age dependency is projected to be offset by declining youth dependency. An assessment of the projected change in tax burden per worker suggests that this is not likely to be so great as to have serious adverse incentive effects.

Indeed, the longer-term historical record raises doubt about fertility leveling off below replacement levels, as currently projected. Completed fertility in this century shows a long-term swing of about fifty years duration, and labor market conditions are now emerging that favor a new upswing. In all of the countries considered here ,the current total fertility rate is above its 1980s trough, and in a number of them the increase is sizable. If a new baby boom were to occur, it would change the dependency outlook in a more favorable direction in the period after 2025, the period when current projections place the dependency burden at its highest. It is hard to understand why the possibility of a new baby boom is so blandly dismissed in demographic projections.

In the literature on less developed countries, recent years have seen a growing skepticism that population growth has important adverse effects on long-term economic growth (see, e.g., Kelley 1986, 1991; U.S. National Research Council 1986). It seems likely that a similar fate is in store for the current literature foreseeing dire consequences for economic growth in the demographic outlook of developed countries.

## References


Bulatao, Rodolfo A., Eduard Bos, Patience W. Stephens, and My T. Vu. 1990. *World Population Projections, 1989-90 Edition.* Baltimore: Johns Hopkins University Press for the World Bank.

Calot, Gerard. 1988. "La Fecondite en Europe: Evolutions Passees et Perspectives d'Avenir." Paper presented at the Symposium on Population Change and European Society, European Institute, Florence, Italy.

Easterlin, Richard A. 1991. "The Economic Impact of Prospective Population Changes in Advanced Industrial Countries: An Historical Perspective," *Journal of Gerontology: Social Sciences* 46, 6 (November): S299–S309.

Holzmann, Robert. 1988. "Ageing and Social-Security Costs," *European Journal of Population* 3:411–437.

Kelley, Allen C. 1986. "Review of National Research Council 'Population Growth and Economic Development: Policy Questions,'" *Population and Development Review* 12:563–568.

_____. 1991. "Revisionism Revisited: An Essay on the Population Debate in Historical Perspective." Paper prepared for the Nobel Jubilee Symposium in Economics, Lund, Sweden, December 5–7.

Klinger, Andras. 1991. "Survey of Recent Fertility Trends and Assumptions Used for Projections." In *Future Demographic Trends in Europe and North America,* Wolfgang Lutz, ed. San Diego: Academic Press.

Maddison, Angus. 1982. *Phases of Capitalist Development.* New York: Oxford University Press.

Monnier, Alain. 1990. "La Conjuncture Demographique: l'Europe et les Pays Developpes d'Outre-Mer," *Population* 4–5 (Juillet-Octobre): 924–936.

Monnier, Alain and Catherine de Guibert-Lantoine. 1991. "La Conjuncture Demographique: l'Europe et les Pays Developpes d'Outre-Mer," *Population* 46, 4 (Juillet-Aout): 941–964.

Organization for Economic Cooperation and Development (OECD). 1983. *Policies for Higher Education in the 1980s.* Paris: OECD.

_____. 1984. *Educational Trends in the 1970s: A Quantitative Analysis.* Paris: OECD.

_____. 1988. *Aging Populations: The Social Policy Implications.* Paris: OECD.

_____. 1990. *Historical Statistics 1960–1988.* Paris: OECD.

_____. Various dates. *Economic Indicator.* Paris: OECD.

*Population Index.* 1948. "The Population Forecasts of the Scripps Foundation," 14, 3: 188–195.

United Nations. 1956. *The Aging of Populations and Its Economic and Social Implication.* New York: United Nations.

_____. 1974. *Demographic Yearbook 1973.* New York: United Nations.

_____. 1980. *Demographic Yearbook 1979.* New York: United Nations.

_____. 1987. *Global Estimates and Projections of Population by Sex and Age.* New York: United Nations.

_____. 1988a. *Economic and Social Implications of Population Aging.* New York: United Nations.

_____. 1988b. *World Demographic Estimates and Projections 1950–2025.* New York: United Nations.

U.S. Bureau of the Census. 1984. *Census of Population 1980. Detailed Population Characteristics.* United States Summary, Section A. Washington, DC: Government Printing Office.

_____. 1987. "An Aging World." International Population Report Series P–95, No. 78. Washington, DC: Government Printing Office.

_____. 1989. *Projections of the Population of the United States by Age, Sex, and Race, 1988 to 2080.* Current Population Reports, Series P–25, No. 1018 (January), by Gregory Spencer. Washington, DC: Government Printing Office.

U.S. National Research Council, Working Group on Population Growth and Economic Development. 1986. *Population Growth and Economic Development: Policy Questions.* Washington, DC: National Academy Press.

Van de Kaa, Dirk. 1988. "The Second Demographic Transition Re-visited: Theories and Expectations." Paper presented at the Symposium on Population Change and European Society, European Institute, Florence, Italy.

Wattenberg, Benjamin. 1987. *The Birth Dearth.* New York: Pharos Books.

World Bank. 1988. *World Development Report 1988.* New York: Oxford University Press.

# Can There Be Too Much Human Capital?

## Is There a World Population Problem?

D. Gale Johnson
*University of Chicago*

Most of the emphasis in the study of human capital is on investment in people and the consequences of that investment—social and private returns, social and private costs, the effects of human capital upon productivity and national output growth, on-the-job training versus formal education, and the substitution between quality and numbers of children. I plan to discuss a rather different aspect of human capital, namely, the value of a person—a human being—with little or no formal investment other than that common in the majority of the developing countries of the world.

My interest in the value of a person whose primary human capital consists of a combination of physical capability, native intelligence, and a limited education investment is in exploring whether population growth has a measurable negative effect upon real per capita income in developing countries. As I use the term, a negative effect exists if the total marginal product of an additional individual is less than the average product of the existing population. This definition of a negative effect does not require that the marginal product be negative, only that it be less than the average product or per capita income level. This is a very stringent test, much stronger than what is generally considered.

I believe if the majority of people were asked what was the relationship between population growth and per capita real incomes in developing countries they would answer that there was a negative relationship—that population growth reduces real per capita incomes below what they would otherwise be. This was the common viewpoint expressed in the popular press prior to and during the 1992 world conference on the environment in Rio de Janeiro. It is the intent of the

Population Crisis Committee, certain agencies of the United Nations, and the authors of *The Population Bomb* to create such an impression. It is certainly the answer given by officials in the People's Republic of China responsible for the country's population programs.

There have been relatively few voices putting forward a contrary view; Julian Simon has been the most prominent. A few years ago (1986) a Working Group was organized by the National Research Council of the National Academy of Sciences, and after many meetings and several studies commissioned, it issued a report (NRC 1986), *Population Growth and Economic Development: Policy Questions,* which has been ignored except for reviews in a few scholarly journals. I hope I will be forgiven if a significant part of this paper is devoted to presenting the major findings of that report which, I believe have stood the test of time very well. But I may be biased—I was the co-chairman of the Working Group.

## Why is Population Growth Bad?

It is useful to start with the arguments that support the view that population growth has adverse effects upon economic growth in developing countries. The case is quite simple and straightforward. The earth is considered to be finite in terms of physical space and resources. The exploitation or use of its resources is subject to diminishing returns—additional inputs (including labor) applied to the land, water, minerals, and forests will yield a diminished return. Therefore, other things equal, more people will mean a reduction in the marginal productivity of labor and, eventually, lower per capita incomes. These relationships seem so obvious that they are seldom spelled out so explicitly. The basic argument hasn't changed from that given by Malthus nearly two centuries ago.

The fact that only a small minority of the world's population eats less well today than did the majority of Europeans at the time Malthus wrote seems not to have dimmed the attractiveness of his model of human behavior (Fogel 1992). It is estimated that in the period 1781–1790, daily per capita calorie consumption in France was 1,753. As of 1965, how many countries in the world had a smaller caloric supply?

The answer is: exactly two—Mozambique and Somalia (World Bank 1992). It was not until the second quarter of the nineteenth century that France's calorie consumption equaled that of India today. At the end of the eighteenth century England's daily per capita production of calories was 10 percent below the Indian daily consumption in 1989. It is sad to note that in 1989 there were three countries, all torn by war and revolution, that had less than 1,753 calories per day—Mozambique, Ethiopia, and Chad—and as of 1992 they have probably been joined by Somalia and Sudan. Yet the view that increased food supplies would soon be followed by increased mouths to feed should not be too surprising, since this view was expressed more than two millennia ago in Ecclesiastes 5.11: "When goods are increased, they are increased that eat them."

The World Bank's *World Development Report 1984* dealt with the issue of population change and development. The discussion, which is both competent and balanced, gave rather little weight to the importance of diminishing returns to or scarcity of resources except for the possible adverse effects of population growth on the environment. Nor was the claim made that rapid population growth stopped development or caused a fall in real per capita income. Instead, the consequences were that rapid population growth, such as that occurring in most developing countries, slowed economic development (p. 105). It attributes the negative effects of rapid population growth to two factors. The first was internal to the family; a large family reduces the investment in each child in terms of time and other resources. Since poor families have the most children, this makes it more difficult to reduce poverty. The second factor was that "rapid population growth weakens macroeconomic performance by making it more difficult to finance the investments in education and infrastructure that ensure sustained economic growth" (p. 105). This work represented an important shift in the scholarly discussion of population growth, but seems not to have penetrated the popular discussion.

## What Are the Facts?

What are the facts concerning the relationship between population growth and development as measured by the growth in real per capita incomes? This may seem like a simple question and, at one level, it is. But as will become clear, it is far from a simple question. Or it may be a simple question with a complex answer or answers.

I shall present some empirical information concerning the relationships between population growth and economic development. Let me note in advance that the empirical relationships presented do not prove causality; they do not prove that population growth has either a positive or negative effect upon development and growth. For this reason the Working Group (NRC 1986) did not present any regressions relating population growth to various variables, such as per capita income growth. Spurious correlations abound. Why do I present such data then? I do so because those who believe that population growth is the source of most human ills either implicitly or explicitly claim that a negative relationship holds between population growth and economic and social development. A recent pamphlet of the Population Crisis Committee, *The International Human Suffering Index,* presents, in color no less, a comparison between an index which it calls the Human Suffering Index and the annual rate of population increase. Two statements are made: "Most countries with high human suffering scores have very high rates of population growth," and "Virtually all the countries with low human suffering scores have low rates of population growth." But there appears to be a very weak statistical relationship between the two variables except between the 57 countries classified as having Minimal and Moderate Human Suffering versus the 83 others. Within the 83 other countries, whose fates include those classified as subject to Extreme Human Suffering, there was almost no relationship between population growth and the index; the square of the correlation coefficient is 0.06. This means that 94 percent of the variation in the suffering index was due to something other than differences in population growth rates. If one's only source of information on the status of the life of people in developing countries were the discussion of the Human Suffering Index, one would hardly guess that life expectancy at birth has increased from no more than 35 years in 1950 to 62 years in 1990 in the low-income countries (less than $600 GNP per capita in 1990).

## Why It Is So Hard To Know

Why is it so hard to determine how population growth affects economic development? As noted, the interrelationships between population and economic growth are very complex. First, if economic development is measured by changes in per capita real income, at certain income levels increases in per capita income will result in an increase in population growth through influences that reduce mortality, especially infant mortality. For the developing economies, there is a strong negative relationship between income levels and infant mortality. Thus, if income and population growth are compared for the same time period, it is likely that there will be a positive relationship between the two. Introducing lags as I have may not entirely eliminate the problems associated with the direction of causality. Second, the effects of population growth can differ in the short and long run, with the short run being perhaps as long as half a century. Other things equal, in the short run an increase in population growth would be expected to lower the rate of growth in real per capita incomes. An increase in population growth rates will be accompanied by an increase in the number of children and in the dependency ratio. The labor force declines as a percentage of the population. In the long run the effects of investment in human capital can be realized. Positive effects through invention and innovation and increasing returns to scale can result from population growth when there is time for adjustment and response to changing conditions. Slow or nil long-run increases in population also increase dependency as the population ages. Thus, in the long run (after one or two generations), slow population growth can have similar effects upon per capita productivity as rapid population growth may have in the short run.

A possible reason for the belief that an increase in population in the developing countries will either lower the actual average income or the rate of growth of income is the implicit assumption that individuals in these countries consume everything they produce. This assumption is incorrect. The people of the developing countries do not consume everything they produce. According to World Bank data (1992, pp. 234–235), the domestic savings rates of the low-income countries are equal to or greater than the rates for either middle- or high-income countries. Thus if resources are productively invested, over a lifetime an additional person would make possible an increase in the productive potential of a country. This conclusion assumes that savings rates are independent of population growth rates, and that point is addressed below. It may be noted that the savings estimate excludes savings that result in human capital investment. If the succeeding generation has more education and more adequate health care than the current generation has, this increases the probability that a significant positive rate of population growth either will have a positive or nil effect on per capita real incomes in the long run. Consequently, in considering the effect of population growth on income growth we must consider the total effect and not solely the marginal product of labor. This is why I earlier used the term "total marginal product" of an additional person which includes not only the marginal product of labor but the increase in investment and any effects through increasing returns to scale.

## Some Empirical Relationships

There are a number of empirical relationships or propositions that merit our attention. The first two are of a very general nature, and the third involves regressions between population growth rates and real per capita incomes with the inclusion of other relevant variables. These empirical propositions raise some questions concerning the validity of the commonly held view that higher rates of population growth have adverse effects upon economic well-being. I do not claim that these empirical relationships imply causality, but only that each is worth pondering and exploring.

The first of the empirical relationships is that the significant increases in the real incomes in the industrial countries of Europe and North America occurred in the eighteenth, nineteenth, and early twentieth centuries during a period of historically rapid population growth that followed a long period of slow population growth. From 1650 to

1750 population growth rates were very low in both the industrial and developing regions at 0.33 and 0.34 percent annually (see table 1). At these rates population doubling would require two centuries. From 1750 to 1900 population growth rates were higher in the industrial than in the developing regions and this difference continued through the first two decades of this century.

**Table 1. Population Growth Rates and Distribution of World Population Between Industrialized and Developing Regions, 1650–1986**

| | Average annual rate | | | | |
|---|---|---|---|---|---|
| Interval | Industrialized regions (B) | Developing regions (A) | Difference (B–A) | % of world pop. in developing regions | % of growth in pop. in developing regions |
| 1980–1986 | 0.66 | 1.98 | -1.32 | 76.9 | 91.6 |
| 1970–1980 | 0.78 | 2.23 | -1.45 | 74.4 | 89.6 |
| 1960–1970 | 1.04 | 2.41 | -1.37 | 71.7 | 86.2 |
| 1950–1960 | 1.26 | 2.07 | -0.81 | 69.9 | 79.8 |
| 1940–1950 | 0.35 | 1.44 | -1.09 | 67.5 | 90.0 |
| 1930–1940 | 0.85 | 1.28 | -0.43 | 66.4 | 77.3 |
| 1920–1930 | 0.91 | 1.11 | -0.20 | 66.1 | 68.6 |
| 1900–1920 | 0.92 | 0.52 | 0.40 | 67.9 | 53.8 |
| 1850–1900 | 1.05 | 0.53 | 0.52 | 73.3 | 54.5 |
| 1800–1850 | 0.83 | 0.31 | 0.52 | 78.1 | 53.4 |
| 1750–1800 | 0.62 | 0.47 | 0.15 | 79.3 | 73.6 |
| 1650–1750 | 0.33 | 0.34 | -0.01 | 79.3 | 79.4 |

SOURCES: Bogue (1969, p. 49); United Nations (1988).

As late as 1840 life expectancy at birth in six European countries and Massachusetts was 41 years (table 2). It reached 50.5 years by 1900 and then increased rapidly reaching 71 years by 1955. While we have little knowledge of life expectancy at birth in the developing regions prior to 1950, it is unlikely that there was any significant improvement in the prior century. However, since 1950 the increase in life expectancy can only be described as spectacular, increasing from 35 years in 1950 to 62 years in 1990 (World Bank 1984 and 1992). Life expectancy at birth in the United States was approximately 42 years in 1880; it did not reach 60 years until 1930. Thus, the lowest income countries in the world achieved a greater increase in life expectancy in 25 years than was achieved in the United States in twice that long. This improvement in the developing regions was achieved during a period of rapid population growth.

**Table 2. Expectation of Life at Birth for Six European Countries and Massachusetts in the United States: 1840 to 1955**

| Year | Expectation of life at birth | Average annual increase in life expectancy |
|---|---|---|
| 1840 | 41.0 | -- |
| 1850 | 41.5 | 0.05 |
| 1860 | 42.2 | 0.07 |
| 1870 | 43.5 | 0.13 |
| 1880 | 45.2 | 0.17 |
| 1890 | 47.1 | 0.20 |
| 1900 | 50.5 | 0.34 |
| 1910 | 54.3 | 0.38 |
| 1920 | 58.3 | 0.40 |
| 1930 | 61.7 | 0.34 |
| 1940 | 64.6 | 0.29 |
| 1955 | 71.0 | 0.43 |

SOURCE: United Nations (1962, table IV.1).

Similar rapid progress has been made in the developing world in reducing infant mortality and child death rates since 1950 (table 3). The infant mortality rate declined from 165 in 1950 to 72 in 1985, while the child death rate fell from 27 to 11; both are rates per 1,000. The infant mortality rate in the United States in 1900 was 160, and it declined to approximately 80 over the next quarter century (U.S. Bureau of the Census 1971, p. 55).

The second of the empirical propositions is that the developing countries had rapid economic growth in the three decades from 1950 to 1980 with population growth rates exceeding those ever realized in the industrial countries. Population growth rates were 2 percent or more while the per capita GDP grew at an annual rate of 2.6 percent during the three decades (National Research Council 1986, p. 5). Prior to 1950 population growth rates had been much lower, generally 1 per-

**Table 3. Life Expectancy at Birth, Infant Mortality Rate, and Child Death Rate**

| Country or income groups[a] | Life expectancy at birth 1960 | Life expectancy at birth 1985[c] | Infant mortality rate[b] (under age 1) 1960 | Infant mortality rate[b] (under age 1) 1985[c] | Child death rate[b] (ages 1–4) 1960 | Child death rate[b] (ages 1–4) 1985[c] | GNP per capita (in $U.S.) 1985[c] |
|---|---|---|---|---|---|---|---|
| Low-income economies | | | | | | | |
| China | 42 | 69 | 165 | 35 | 26 | 7 | 310 |
| India | 43 | 56 | 165 | 89 | 26 | 11 | 270 |
| Other | 43 | 52 | 163 | 112 | 31 | 19 | 200 |
| Average | 42 | 60 | 165 | 72 | 27 | 11 | 270 |
| Africa | | | | | | | |
| Low-income | | | | | | | |
| Semi-arid | 37 | 44 | 203 | 151 | 57 | 34 | 218 |
| Other | 39 | 49 | 158 | 112 | 37 | 22 | 254 |
| Average | 38 | 48 | 164 | 117 | 40 | 24 | 249 |
| Middle-income | | | | | | | |
| Oil importers | 41 | 50 | 159 | 111 | 37 | 21 | 670 |
| Oil exporters | 39 | 50 | 191 | 113 | 51 | 21 | 889 |
| Sub-Saharan | -- | 49 | 170 | 115 | 42 | 23 | 491 |
| Middle-income economies | 51 | 62 | 126 | 68 | 23 | 10 | 1,290 |
| Lower-middle income | 46 | 58 | 144 | 82 | 29 | 13 | 820 |
| Upper-middle income | 56 | 66 | 101 | 52 | 15 | 6 | 1,850 |
| Industrial market economies | 70 | 76 | 29 | 9 | 2 | -- | 11,810 |

SOURCE: World Bank (1987).

a. Income designations are based on per capita income (in 1985 U.S. dollars): low income, $390 or less; lower-middle income, $400–$1,600; upper-middle income, $1,600–$7,420.

b. Rates are per 1,000.

c. Data for Africa are for 1982.

cent or less, and there had been slow or nil increases in real per capita incomes.

Economic growth was relatively slow during the 1950s in the low-income countries. If we look at a somewhat later period, 1965 to 1985, the rate of income growth was quite spectacular. The per capita gross national product for the low-income countries grew 2.9 percent annually for 1965–85 and exceeded the 2.4 percent of the industrial economies (World Bank 1987). Since low-income countries were defined as those with less than $400 per capita GNP in 1985, some rapidly growing countries that were poor in 1965 were excluded from the calculation because they grew out of the low-income category by 1985; had these countries been included, the growth of income would have been even higher.

The third of the empirical propositions is that the evidence does not support the view that for developing countries the rate of population growth has a negative effect upon per capita income growth for the period since 1950. Some results are given in table 4 for three decades. In the simple model it was assumed that per capita income growth in a decade was a function of population growth and per capita income growth in the prior decade. Enrollment ratios for primary schools and per capita gross domestic products were included. School enrollment is included to provide a rough indication of society's investment in human capital. Per capita GDP is included to determine if there is a convergence effect among the developing countries. Per capita GDP growth in the prior decade was included because of the possible causality between income growth and population growth and the possibility of continuity in per capita income growth from one decade to the next. The coefficient for population growth was positive but not significantly different from zero for each of the three decades for low-income countries. For middle-income countries the coefficient was negative and significantly different from zero at the 10 percent level for the 1960s, but was not significant for either of the other two decades. Thus, of the six coefficients for the developing countries, only one indicated that there was a (weak) negative relationship between past population growth and current growth of GDP per capita. The variables included had surprisingly little relationship to the real per capita growth rates. The correlation coefficients were very small and none of the coefficients were statistically significant at the conventional 5 percent level. Obviously other variables, including policy variables, are much more important in influencing income growth rates than population growth or the human capital measures that I have included.

**Table 4. Cross-Country Regressions of Per Capita GDP Growth Rates**

| **Low income** | **1960–1970** | **1970–1980** | **1980–1988** |
|---|---|---|---|
| Lagged population growth | 0.053 | 0.115 | 0.319 |
| Enrollment primary school | -0.015 | 0.025 | -0.015 |
| Lagged GDP growth | 0.226 | -0.221 | -0.286 |
| Lagged GDP level | -0.001 | -0.003* | 0.000 |
| Dummy: Africa | -0.931 | -0.742 | -3.371* |
| $\overline{R}^2$ | -0.004 | 0.163 | 0.059 |
| n | 12 | 32 | 33 |
| **Middle income** | | | |
| Lagged population growth | -0.524** | 0.319 | -0.551 |
| Enrollment primary school | 0.017 | 0.029 | 0.024 |
| Lagged GDP growth | 0.236 | 0.163 | 0.320* |
| Lagged GDP level | -0.005 | 0.000 | 0.000** |
| Dummy: Africa | -0.711 | -0.241 | -0.792 |
| Latin America | -0.859 | -0.608 | -2.115** |
| $\overline{R}^2$ | 0.163 | -0.043 | 0.055 |
| n | 32 | 61 | 58 |

NOTES: GDP data are from Summers and Heston (1991); and World Bank (various years). Lagged population and lagged GDP growth rates are for the prior decade; lagged GDP level is beginning year of the decade. Africa and Latin America dummies are 1 for country in region, 0 otherwise. Constant terms not presented.
*Statistically significant at 5 percent level.
**Statistically significant at 10 percent level.

Table 5 is from Levine and Renelt (1992), who included population growth as one of the variables in their analysis of the influence of policy factors on economic growth in 119 countries. In none of the regressions was there a statistically significant effect of population growth on the rate of economic growth. Several of the policy or policy-related variables had a statistically significant coefficient, especially investment and government share. A study by Singh (1992) for twenty-nine developing economies obtained negative but insignificant coefficients

**Table 5. Cross-Country Growth Regressions (Dependent Variable: Growth Rate of Real Per Capita GDP)**

| | Regression period data set | | | | |
|---|---|---|---|---|---|
| **Independent variable** | **1960–1989 WB/IMF (1)** | **1960–1985 SH (2)** | **1960–1989 WB/IMF (3)** | **1960–1985 WB/IMF (4)** | **1960–1985 SH (5)** |
| Constant | -0.83 | 2.01 | 0.86 | 0.47 | 2.05 |
| | (0.85) | (0.83) | (0.89) | (1.18) | (1.12) |
| Initial GDP per capita (RGDP60) | -0.35* | -0.69* | -0.30* | -0.40* | -0.57* |
| | (0.14) | (0.12) | (0.11) | (0.13) | (0.12) |
| Investment share (INV) | 17.49* | 9.31* | 16.77* | 13.44* | 10.15* |
| | (2.68) | (2.08) | (2.62) | (3.13) | (2.43) |
| Population growth (GPO) | -0.38 | 0.08 | -0.53 | -0.15 | -0.02 |
| | (0.22) | (0.18) | (0.18) | (0.19) | (0.19) |
| Secondard-school enrollment (SEC) | 3.17* | 1.21 | | 0.63 | 0.99 |
| | (1.29) | (1.17) | | (1.26) | (1.23) |
| Primary-school enrollment (PRI) | | 1.79* | | 0.91 | 1.07 |
| | | (0.58) | | (0.73) | (0.70) |
| Government share (GOV) | | -6.37* | | -0.59 | -6.80* |
| | | (2.03) | | (3.73) | (2.30) |
| Growth of government share (GSG) | | | -0.08 | | |
| | | | (0.06) | | |
| Socialist economy (SOC) | | -0.25 | | -0.21 | -0.17 |
| | | (0.38) | | (0.45) | (0.43) |

| | (1) | (2) | (3) | (4) | (5) |
|---|---|---|---|---|---|
| Revolution/coups (REVC) | | -1.76* | | -0.86 | -1.75* |
| | | (0.52) | | (0.62) | (0.59) |
| Africa dummy (AFRICA) | | -1.24* | | -1.36* | -1.78* |
| | | (0.37) | | (0.48) | (0.44) |
| Latin America dummy (LAAM) | | -1.18* | | -1.34* | -1.27* |
| | | (0.33) | | (0.38) | (0.36) |
| Growth of domestic credit (GDC) | | | 0.019* | 0.013 | 0.008 |
| | | | (0.009) | (0.008) | (0.007) |
| Standard deviation of domestic credit (STDD) | | | -0.009* | -0.006* | -0.003 |
| | | | (0.003) | (0.003) | (0.003) |
| Civil liberties (CIVL) | | | -0.22 | 0.01 | 0.15 |
| | | | (0.11) | (0.13) | (0.13) |
| Export-share growth (XSG) | | | 0.090 | 0.023 | -0.03 |
| | | | (0.052) | (0.047) | (0.041) |
| Number of observations | 101 | 103 | 83 | 84 | 86 |
| $\bar{R}^2$ | 0.46 | 0.68 | 0.61 | 0.67 | 0.73 |

SOURCE: Levine and Renelt (1992).

NOTES: Regressions (1), (3), and (4) use primarily World Bank and IMF data, while regressions (2) and (5) use Summers and Heston data. Coverage includes all countries with data given by the sources except major oil exporters.

*Statistically significant at the P=0.05 level.

for the population growth variable. In each of these studies the periods for income and population growth were contemporaneous.

## Population Growth Only One Factor

Before summarizing the results of the NRC study on population growth and economic development, I want to make a point that is all too often ignored in the popular discussions of the subject. Population growth is only one factor in determining the economic well-being of the citizens of a country. And, looking around the world today at the observed differences in real per capita incomes, it seems to be a rather minor factor in explaining such differences. Governmental policies are of far greater importance. Much of the human suffering witnessed in recent years has not been caused by excessive population growth or too large populations; most of the real causes are to be found in civil war and strife and governmental mismanagement and failures. Bangladesh is a probable exception to this conclusion, but I am not sure that there are any others.

China is a clear example of the dominance of factors other than population growth in explaining real income growth over the past four decades. While there has been a reduction in population growth rates over the past three decades, the small decline in the population growth rate after the early 1970s can't account for any significant part of the sharp changes in the growth of income per capita. Using the Summers and Heston (1991) estimates, per capita GDP grew at an annual rate of 2.3 percent from 1960–1973, by 3.7 percent from 1973–1980 and, during major policy reforms, 7.8 percent from 1980 to 1988. Population growth rates in Taiwan closely parallel those of the mainland, but from 1960 to 1980 the real income growth rate was double that of the mainland. This difference can only be explained by policy factors. From 1980–1988 the per capita income growth rate on the mainland exceeded that of Taiwan.

Most African countries, unfortunately, provide further evidence of how the national policy framework dominates changes in economic welfare. From 1973–1980, thirty out of forty-six African countries had negative real per capita income growth rates (Summers and Heston

1991). The same number had negative per capita growth rates during 1980–1988. During these two periods the African countries generally followed import substitution policies with heavy taxation of agriculture, especially of export commodities. The beginning of the shift to market-oriented policies did not begin generally until the mid-1980s and is just now beginning to influence the pattern of growth.

## Propositions: Population and Growth

In the report, *Population Growth and Economic Development: Policy Questions* (NRC 1986), nine questions were posed and the available evidence was used to answer them. I shall now paraphrase the nine questions and provide a brief summary of the report's conclusions.

1. Would slower population growth increase the per capita supply of exhaustible resources?

In reflecting upon this question, it should be remembered that over the past century the real prices of exhaustible natural resources have declined, not increased (Simon 1981). The decline in the prices of such resources relative to wages or earnings has been striking; for oil and coal the time cost today is about a fifth of what it was a century ago. The same pattern of decline in relative scarcity has prevailed for nonfuel resources such as copper.

An important point is that no exhaustible resource is essential or irreplaceable. As the easily available supplies of such a resource are extracted, the real cost of extraction and the price increase, which encourages economy in the use of that resource and stimulate the search for substitutes. One reason that real copper prices have declined is that aluminum, which is derived from a plentiful resource (bauxite), has been substituted for it in many uses, especially wire.

A little reflection will convince you that the number of people who will enjoy the use of an exhaustible resource will be the same whether population growth is slow or fast. Exhaustion will occur sooner with rapid population growth than with slow population growth, but the number of people who will have used the resource will be the same. If you contend that with more time provided by slower population growth it would be possible to learn how to economize on the use of the resource, you have already lost most of your argument that rapid population growth results in undue resource exhaustion. The application of more resources to find ways to economize on use of the exhaustible resource is an effective substitute for more time. With a larger population there are more human resources to devote to the problem at an earlier time.

2. Would slower population growth increase the per capita availability of renewable resources and thus increase per capita income?

Up to the present, the decline in the per capita availability of renewable resources, such as land, has not resulted in a reduction in per capita income. Instead, the long-run trend in the prices of farm products that depend upon land, especially the food crops, has been a declining one over the past century (Simon 1981).

We need to bear in mind that the use of renewable resources is influenced by existing institutional arrangements. Some institutional arrangements, such as common property or property rights, that are limited and uncertain may have disastrous effects upon the conservation of renewable resources. Consider the near extinction of certain kinds of whales or the depletion of certain fishing areas. These occurred where common property existed and, until recently, no effective mechanism existed for avoiding the "tragedy of the commons." The tragedy of the commons occurs because it is in the interest of the individual to use or harvest the commons as long as what is harvested has a value greater than the costs, even though this activity reduces the total output. Consequently, if serious problems do occur due to the diminution of the productivity of renewable resources, it will probably be because appropriate institutional arrangements do not exist.

3. Will slower population growth alleviate pollution and environmental degradation?

Environmental resources, such as air and water, are almost always common property; unless appropriate institutional arrangements exist, these resources will be overused whether population is growing rapidly, slowly, or not at all. There is an optimum level of pollution, namely, the level at which the marginal cost of reducing the pollution equals the value of the marginal harm done by the pollutant. But where air or water are common property, no enterprise or person has to bear more than a small part of the cost of pollution created. Public policy has the responsibility of internalizing the cost of pollution by adopting measures, such as regulations, fees, or incentives for pollution abatement, that force or induce producers to limit the amount of pollution to the socially optimum level. Please note that enterprise is used here in a very broad sense and includes enterprises owned publicly, such as the Tennessee Valley Authority or the local school district, as well as those owned privately; no form of ownership has a monopoly on pollution.

Major sources of pollution in the world today, however, are not associated with rapidly growing populations but with either populations with high incomes or in countries that had socialist economic systems. Feshback and Friendly (1992) chronicle the story of how having the means of production "owned by all the people" led to environmental disaster in the Soviet Union. People with high incomes consume more than people with low incomes, and their demands upon production resources and the potential for environmental disruption are greater. It follows that if population growth has little or no effect on income growth, more people increase the potential for environmental disruption; but the actual amount of environmental disruption is a function of many variables other than either per capita incomes or population.

Based on research done since 1986, it is now possible to say more about the effects of developing country economic growth on the state of the environment. A major factor in economic growth is the openness of the economy to the world economy—the degree of trade liberalization. Because of the comments about the North American Free Trade Agreement by groups that the press calls environmentalists, I start by noting the probable effects of world trade liberalization upon the environment. This is a topic ably addressed in a recent paper by Kym Anderson (1992).

The probable direct effect of world trade liberalization would be to reduce pollution overall. Two effects are worthy of note. Agriculture is an important source of ground water pollution, especially in the industrial countries. This is due to the relatively heavy use of chemicals in crop production and the concentration of livestock production in large units. Trade liberalization for farm products would shift crop production from countries with high farm output prices and heavy chemical use to countries that have and would continue to have lower levels of fertilizer and pesticide use. If there were worldwide trade liberalization in agricultural products, grain production would shift from Western Europe to Argentina, Australia, Thailand, and the United States. With the lower crop prices in Western Europe, chemical use would be significantly reduced. While use of chemicals would increase some in the countries expanding crop production, the use level would be relatively low due to the price relationships between crops and fertilizer. The expansion in U.S. crop production would result from the return of idled land to cultivation; chemical use would fall.

The second direct effect of trade liberalization relates to the use of energy. Most developing countries hold energy prices below world market prices, resulting in excessive use of energy per unit of output. In China and India coal prices have been kept at hardly more than half the world market prices. Not only is an excessive amount of coal and other energy used, but energy is used inefficiently because it has not paid to invest in new and less polluting combustion technology. Inefficiency in combustion leads to a high level of pollution per btu consumed.

If the developing countries liberalize trade, including trade in energy, energy prices will rise to world market levels and there will be an incentive to conserve in the use of energy and thus reduce pollution.

One of the sources of environmental disruption in the low-income developing countries is the harvesting of forests for firewood and the consequent erosion and silting of rivers. As labor becomes more valuable, wood becomes less competitive as fuel. Its main cost under the conditions in the low-income developing countries is time, since the institutional arrangements permit harvesting without paying for the trees. Deforestation occurs not only because labor is so cheap, but because the rights to utilize the forest are not well defined.

The available evidence indicates that pollution abatement is a normal good. This means that the income elasticity of demand for pollution abatement is positive and that as real per capita incomes increase, people demand more pollution abatement. It is not only that more effort and resources are devoted to pollution abatement, but the acceptable standards for pollution become more stringent. Consequently, it can be expected that as per capita incomes increase in the developing countries, less and less pollution will be acceptable and permitted. Restraints on pollution are a function of per capita incomes, population density, and urbanization.

Those who opposed NAFTA because of presumed environmental effects apparently failed to consider such rational responses. Theirs is a highly condescending and even insulting view of the people of developing countries. The progress that developing countries have made in environmental improvement where it really counts, namely, in saving lives, has been enormous over the past four decades. Earlier I referred to the sharp reduction in infant mortality. A large share of this decline resulted from environmental improvements—better handling of sewage and the provision of safer and cleaner water. These changes occurred because the people of the developing countries had more income and allocated increased resources to improving their environment. And the evidence is clear: they have been highly successful at improving the environment where it really counts in saving lives and reducing illness.

4. Will slower population growth lead to more capital per worker and higher per capita worker output and income?

Does slower population growth increase the rate of saving? The NRC (1986) Working Group, after reviewing various ways in which population growth could influence the savings rate, concluded: "We have found little evidence that the aggregate savings rate depends on growth rates or the age structure of the population" (p. 87). Subsequently, A.C. Kelley (1988) presented the results of his research on the effect of population growth on savings and investments in developing countries. He considered three possible reasons for negative effects upon economic growth: age dependency, capital shallowing, and investment diversion. The age dependency effect is due to the large proportion of children who do not work; the children may also be responsible for investment diversion to consumption. Capital shallowing is nothing more than a reduction in the amount of capital per worker if savings decline on a per capita basis. Kelley concluded that the empirical research had not substantiated any of these effects (p. 459). He also noted that where the economic analysis was rather more sophisticated and included second order effects such as economizing on resources and supply effects, the "puzzle of reconciling the apparent divergencies between theory and fact disappears" (p. 460).

5. Do lower population densities cause lower per capita incomes by reduced stimulus to innovation and reduced economies of scale?

One of Adam Smith's greatest contributions to economics was his analysis of the interrelationships between specialization, the extent of the market, and the existence of economies of scale. The NRC Working Group concluded that for manufacturing, the economies of scale can be achieved at an unspecified moderate-sized city. The liberalization of international trade in agricultural products and the international flow of capital and technology probably does mean that low rates of population growth are without significant effect upon innovation in manufacturing productivity. And the same answer seems to apply if the question is put differently: Does rapid population growth reduce the growth of labor productivity in manufacturing? The answer also seems to be in the negative.

The Working Group concluded that low density of population could and probably did have adverse effects upon productivity in agriculture. This effect resulted from the costs of the infrastructure, such as roads, communication, marketing services, agricultural research and extension. While Boserup (1981) showed how increased population density influenced the intensity of cultivation and encouraged technological change, it cannot be ruled out that after a certain density of agricultural population is reached, the productivity effects of increased density are either nil or negative. This still seems to be an open question.

6. Will slower population growth increase per capita levels of schooling and health?

This question needs to be considered in two parts. The first is the effect of an increase in the average number of children in a family upon family expenditures on education and schooling. The evidence supports the conclusion that having more children reduces the amount spent on each child.

The second part is the response of the public sectors to an increase in the number of children. T.P. Schultz (1987) found that the percentage of school-age children enrolled in school was not associated with the size of the school-age population relative to the total population. He found, however, that expenditures per child were a negative function of the relative size of the school-age population. These results are quite striking; they indicate that during recent years of rapidly growing populations in developing countries, these countries were able to increase the places in school rapidly enough to keep pace. In fact, in almost all developing countries the percentage of school-age children in school has increased. Increasing the number of places, unfortunately, was apparently associated with little increase in total expenditures on education as the percentage of the population in school increased.

The Working Group could not isolate any effects of population growth on health expenditures due to the poor quality of the available data.

7. Will slower population growth decrease the degree of income inequality?

In the short run the effects of slower population growth on income inequality depend on the distribution of the fertility decline among income groups. If the fertility decline occurs first in the higher income groups, the short-run effects will be to increase the inequality of the income distribution. If the fertility decline is greater in urban than in rural areas, there will be a short-run increase in income inequality, since urban incomes are significantly higher than rural incomes in developing countries

In the long run the effect of a decline in fertility on the distribution of income is likely to work through increasing the amount of capital per worker as the number of entrants to the labor force declines. This conclusion depends on the earlier conclusion that savings rates are independent of population growth or age composition. In effect, if labor becomes more scarce, it may command a higher share of the national product and in this way somewhat reduce the inequality in the distribution of income.

8. Will slower population growth facilitate the transfer of workers into the modern sector and alleviate problems of urban growth?

It cannot be doubted that rapid urbanization has occurred in the developing countries since 1950, nor can one doubt that the rapid growth was a response to population growth rates. Approximately 60 percent of the increase in urban population has been due to natural population growth; the remainder has been due to migration from rural areas (NRC 1986, p. 67).

But once these facts are noted, it is important to recognize that part of the rapid growth of cities such as Mexico City and Cairo has been due to policies that subsidized living in cities, especially by providing large food subsidies that in most cases were not available to farmers. In addition, the income differences between urban and rural populations in developing countries have been very large, generally with urban per capita incomes ranging from 2.5 to 5 times rural incomes. Often the low rural incomes have reflected an urban bias, as well as the taxation of agriculture through low prices for farm products and high prices for farm inputs.

Consequently, governmental policies have had a role in rapid urbanization in the developing countries. If agriculture and rural areas were permitted to share more fully in economic growth, there would be less concern about too rapid urbanization. But economic growth does result in a shift of population from rural to urban areas, and this shift can be avoided only at large cost. Except to protect the relatively high incomes of those now in the cities, it is not obvious why there should be objection to the growth of urban populations.

9. Can a couple's fertility behavior impose costs on society at large?

The apparent answer is in the affirmative. Where there are public goods such as parks and roads, another child increases congestion. Given that most schools are publicly financed, an additional child imposes costs upon taxpayers generally. Furthermore, additional children will in due course increase the number of workers and thus reduce wages, resulting in a potential increase in income inequality. This is essentially the answer in the NRC Working Group report.

It was an answer that I found unconvincing because it ignored the general thrust of the report, namely, that population growth had little or no effect on per capita income growth. True, some negative effects were noted, such as on the quality of education or at least on per capital education expenditures. But there were also some positive effects, such as economies of scale. On balance it seems to me that there is little evidence to support the position that a family imposes net negative externalities upon society when it chooses to have another child. The family does impose certain costs upon others, but the most important of these—the cost of schooling—is a cost that most societies have chosen to bear publicly for the general benefits that a society derives from having a well-educated population.

At least the Working Group came down against governmental coercion to control fertility decisions, although it was unwilling to use the word coercion and instead said that it preferred using changes in incentives rather than quantity rationing. Quantity rationing—limiting the number of children a couple may have—can only be imposed by the application of coercion. Finally, the following was stated: "It is important to note, however, that current data and theory are inadequate to quantify the size of the external effects; certainly there is no evidence to suggest that drastic financial or legal restrictions on child bearing are warranted" (p. 84).

## What is the Value of a Person?

The last of the questions concerning whether an added birth imposes costs upon society generally, is not quite the question that I posed at the beginning of this paper. The question I posed was whether adding to the population lowered the level of per capita income. Put another way, the question was whether in a developing country the total marginal product of a person of average human capital was below the average product of that economy. I interpret the evidence, including the research and conclusions of the Working Group, to support the conclusion that the population growth rates that we have observed in recent decades have had little or no significant effect upon the level or the rate of growth of per capita income in either the long or the short run.

I wish to note two caveats to the conclusion that I have just stated. First, there are reasons to argue that moderate rates of population growth are more supportive of economic development than either low, including negative, or high rates. I define moderate rates of population growth in the approximate range of 1.25 to 2.5 percent. Population growth rates of 3 percent or more may reduce rates of per capita income growth primarily because of the stress placed upon institutions, such as education, health, and city governments, by the high rates of adjustment required. High rates of population growth may require rates of response that are beyond the capabilities of such institutions. Second, even if population growth rates have no significant effects upon economic development, governments should pursue many ordinary economic and social programs, such as universal elementary education, maternal and child health care, and institutions that assist individuals in providing personal financial security, that have the effect of reducing the rates of population growth, although that is not the primary objective of such programs.

## A Positive Population Policy

I strongly support a positive population policy that seeks the objective of assisting every family in a country to have the number of children that each family desires. By definition, such programs must be voluntary; coercion and compulsion are simply not consistent with each family achieving its objectives. Thus I strongly favor governments making both relevant information and contraceptive materials available to every family that desires such information and materials. As I argued above, a case has not been made that there is a significantly negative externality to the number of children a family has. But, because I believe that the welfare of families is enhanced if they are given the resources that they need to limit the number of children to the number each family desires, I believe that governments should accept the responsibility of assuring that such resources are available and their availability is highly publicized.

I would argue that governments should go well beyond what many would argue is a passive population policy such as I have described, though in most real world situations policy makers would not agree that such a policy can be carried out without addressing some real conflicts. While ruling out coercion, governments can and do influence the number of children a family desires as well as the number a family has. This can be done by influencing conditions that are recognized to have an effect upon the number of children desired. Education, especially of women, has major impacts on both the desired and the actual number of children. Creating conditions that reduce infant mortality leads to a reduction in the number of children born, though with a lag.

In many rural communities old-age security is achieved primarily through having several children, especially male children. In rural China, for example, the rural reforms have not produced any alternative sources of old-age security to having one or more sons. While the ownership of land is one means for providing security in one's older years, private ownership of farm land does not exist in China. Not only can rural families not own the land they farm, they cannot assume that the land use rights assigned to them can be readily marketed. There are other alternatives for making provision for the uncertainties of old age and death, such as life insurance and access to reliable savings institutions that are allowed to have positive real interest rates. The most immediate and direct approach for the provision of old-age security in China would be the extension of the social security system to the entire population, rather than restricting it to the employees of the government and state and some collective enterprises.

The cost of providing a pension to all rural residents 65 years and older at 80 percent of the average annual income of all rural residents would not be beyond the financial resources of the Chinese government. In 1989 there were 56 million persons living outside of cities who were 65 years of age or older. If the average pension were 50 yuan per month, the annual cost would be 34 billion yuan. This is less than the budgetary cost of the grain price subsidy in 1991! This subsidy went to urban residents who, on average, had far higher incomes than rural people. It appears that the grain price subsidy is being phased out. It would be hard to think of any alternative use for those funds that would create greater happiness and contribute more to the future viability and tranquility of the Chinese society than the creation of a universal social security system.

Such a system, especially if combined with providing the institutional and legal framework for individuals to make some provision for their financial security, would achieve two major objectives. It would significantly alter the incentives to have large numbers of children, and it would reduce the neglect and mistreatment of female babies. Put more directly, much of the pressure in rural China for violating the restraints of the coercive population policy would be eliminated if rural families had viable alternatives to a son or sons to provide security for their old age.

Coercive population programs do great harm, not only to families but to a nation. Fortunately, policies and programs that will lead to reductions in population growth rates need not be coercive. The appropriate criteria for evaluating programs that directly influence the number of births is the degree to which families are assisted in having the number of children they desire. Lacking evidence that family decisions with respect to the number of children have adverse external effects upon others, there is no basis for coercive behavior by governments. Even if there were some adverse external effects, however, I would still hold that decisions with respect to the number of children should be made by the family. It is difficult to imagine that anyone who accepts the Western concept of human rights would approve of the use of coercive restraints placed on such a fundamental right.

## References

Anderson, Kym. 1992. "Economic Growth, Environmental Issues and Trade." Twentieth PAFTAD Conference, Washington, DC, September 10–12.

Bogue, Donald J. 1969. *Principles of Demography.* New York: Wiley.

Boserup, Esther. 1981. *Population and Technological Change.* Chicago: University of Chicago Press.

Feshback, Murray, and Alfred Friendly, Jr. 1992. *Ecocide in the USSR.* New York: Basic Books.

Fogel, Robert. 1992. "Egalitarianism: The Economic Revolution of the Twentieth Century." Unpublished paper, 1992 Simon Kuznets Memorial Lectures, Yale University, April 22–24.

Johnson, D. Gale, and Ronald D. Lee, eds. 1987. *Population Growth and Economic Development: Issues and Evidence.* Madison: University of Wisconsin Press.

Kelley, Allen C. 1988. "Population Pressures, Saving, and Investment in the Third World: Some Puzzles," *Economic Development and Cultural Change* 36, 3: 449–64.

Levine, Ross, and David Renelt. 1992. "A Sensitivity Analysis of Cross-Country Growth Regressions," *American Economic Review* 82, 4: 942–63.

National Research Council (NRC). 1986. *Population Growth and Economic Development: Policy Questions,* Working Group on Population and Economic Development, Washington, DC: National Academy Press.

Population Crisis Committee. 1992. *The International Human Suffering Index.* Washington, DC: Population Crisis Committee.

Schultz, T. Paul. 1987. "School Expenditures and Enrollments, 1960–80: The Effects of Income, Prices and Population Growth." In *Population Growth and Development: Issues and Evidence,* D. Gale Johnson and Ronald D. Lee, eds. Madison: University of Wisconsin Press, pp. 413–76.

Simon, Julian L. 1981. *The Ultimate Resource.* Princeton: Princeton University Press.

_____. 1986. *Theory of Population and Economic Growth.* New York: Basil Blackwell.

Singh, Ram D. 1992. "Government Induced Price Distortions and Growth: Evidence from Twenty-Nine Developing Countries," *Public Choice* 73: 83–99.

Summers, Robert, and Alan Heston. 1991. "The Penn World Table (Mark 5): An Expanded Set of International Comparisons, 1950–1988," *Quarterly Journal of Economics* 107, 2: 327–368.

United Nations. 1962. *Population Bulletin No. 6.* New York: United Nations.

_____. 1988. *Demographic Yearbook 1986.* New York: United Nations.

United States Bureau of the Census. 1971. *Statistical Abstract of the United States.* Washington, DC: Government Printing Office.

World Bank. Various years. *World Development Report.* New York: Oxford University Press.

# Human Capital Accumulation, the Family, and Economic Development

Mark R. Rosenzweig
*University of Pennsylvania*

Family issues—particularly the notion that there has been a decline in "family values" as signaled, for example, by a lack of respect for elders and family instability—have become an important theme of political debates in the United States in recent times. Another important theme has been the relationship between economic development and human capital investment. This essay is concerned with the relationships between human capital, the family, and economic development. In particular, it examines two related questions: First, do family arrangements and family stability, as characterized by the structure of households and their dissolution and marital patterns, reflect the rapidity of economic development, such that enhanced growth and development can cause a "breakdown" of the family? Second, how does economic development affect the returns to and investments in different types of human capital? I will attempt to show that these two questions are linked, that the technological transformation of an economy, by altering the value of different kinds of human capital and increasing incomes, also affects the nature and stability of family relationships.

To understand the complex relationships among growth, human capital, and the family would be quite difficult in the context of an economy such as that of the United States. Distinguishing the effects of development on the returns to human capital investments from the effects of human capital investments on development, for example, is a formidable task. Moreover, the measurement of economic growth and the technical change that underlies it is fraught with difficulties when the economy is as technologically differentiated as in the United States. As a consequence, I look for some answers to the questions about the family-human capital-growth nexus in a simpler economy, that of rural India.

There are three key reasons for studying the Indian rural economy to understand better the relationships between family, human capital, and development. First, that economy is relatively homogenous with respect to production compared to the United States. The most important economic activity by far is agricultural production, and as a consequence it is easier to characterize the economic constraints facing individuals and households.

Second, an important and recent source of economic development in India is clear—the "green revolution." There is no question that a major source of rural development and growth was technical change that was essentially exogenous to the Indian economy. In particular, the widespread availability of substantially more productive varieties of wheat and rice, which began in the early and mid-1960s, was not due to increases in human capital investments or to changes in family arrangements in rural areas. Moreover, because the technological change was crop-specific, not all of the Indian economy could benefit directly from the new grain varieties. The geographically selective nature of the green revolution and its relatively clear timing means that we have a natural experiment in which we can compare, before and after the technical change began, areas now experiencing growth propelled by agricultural technical change with those areas without such growth.

The third and essential reason for examining the Indian economy is that there are excellent data describing that economy. We can thus exploit the green revolution experiment. In particular, there are two sets of data that (1) characterize the behavior of Indian farmers over time in an environment relatively untouched by the green revolution, and (2) describe farmers across all of India, both within and outside of green revolution areas. Thus there is information that describes family arrangements, schooling, and agricultural production prior to and after the onset of technical change in the same areas, as well as in areas without significant agricultural productivity growth.

I use results from prior studies undertaken by me and others over the last decade based on these data describing Indian farm families to examine hypotheses about families and the role of human capital as affected by economic growth. First, I will briefly discuss the key features of undeveloped agricultural economies typical of a low-income country such as India prior to the green revolution, how these characteristics influence family arrangements and stability and the value of human capital, and how technological change affects these factors. I will then describe the data sets and what they say about the characteristics of families and households and related behaviors that require explanation. This section is followed by an examination of the evidence pertaining to specific hypotheses about the relationship between human capital returns and family structures and arrangements under a no-growth, low-income regime, with particular attention to risk mitigation and experience as human capital. I then turn to an examination of the evidence on how agricultural technical change affects human capital investments and family structure, and conclude with some speculations about the policy implications of the results.

## Hypotheses About Family Arrangements and Human Capital Returns in Agricultural Settings

### *The Agricultural Environment Prior to Technical Change*

The four most important features of the environment experienced by agricultural households in a setting without technical advances are: (1) intertemporal variability in rainfall, a critical productive input; (2) spatial covariability in rainfall—families living close-by experience similar weather at the same time; (3) stationarity in weather, making it possible to assess weather risk and the consequences of weather, once realized, for production and income; and (4) the absence of insurance for adverse rainfall conditions or shortfalls in incomes. As a consequence of fluctuating rainfall, and other weather conditions, households experience fluctuating incomes and have a need for mechanisms, alternative to formal insurance, to smooth their consumption.

There are two principal means of consumption-smoothing. Farmers can attempt to reduce the impact of weather variation on incomes by altering their productive practices or inputs prior to the realization of rainfall, by installing irrigation facilities, for example.[1] These *ex ante* adjustments to the riskiness of rainfall can be supplemented by attempts to transfer income from good-weather periods to bad-weather periods by *ex post* adjustment to realized weather outcomes. Saving, by storing output, or borrowing from the more fortunate are examples. Note, however, that neighbors are of limited help in bad-weather times, as they are likely to experience shortfalls at the same time as the "distressed" household because of the covariant nature of rainfall.

In this economy, experience is the most valuable form of human capital. Given the stationarity of weather, farmers learn over time the best ways of coping *ex ante* and *ex post* with the varieties of rainfall based on their experience. Moreover, if land plots are differentiated, the returns to such experience are specific to plots of land or the local economy. As a consequence, schooling, which enables farmers to acquire knowledge outside their immediate environment, provides little return. Because of stationarity, traditional practices based on years of experience (learning by doing) are optimal, with book knowledge about other environments of little value.

Where experience is valuable, the elderly have the highest levels of human capital; it would be expected in such stationary environments that elders would be "respected." In particular, where the returns to plot-specific experience are high, there are incentives for children and parents to farm together on the family land. By working on the family land, the children acquire specific knowledge about that land, and that land then becomes more valuable to them than any other land in the economy and is worth more to them than to any anonymous agent. The children will thus want to remain on the family land that they will inherit. The gains from keeping the land within the family, arising from plot-specific experience, are shared intergenerationally, with the adult children perhaps working at lower rates of pay than hired laborers or working harder in exchange for future returns they will earn on the family land from their experience on it. Thus, the existence of experiential returns leads to intergenerational co-production and to little land divestment. Family stability with highly valued elders should be characteristic of the stationary but risky traditional economy.[2]

Note that this plot-specific experience hypothesis turns the "old-age security" hypothesis on its head—the vertical extension of farm households is not due to the need by the elders for support from their more productive children, but rather reflects the enhanced value of the elders' human capital, relative to their children, which is tied to the family land. The value of accumulated experience as a factor in binding together two generations of family members also implies that there is no reason for adult siblings to co-produce after their father dies. Each sibling essentially brings no additional embodied knowledge to the farming enterprise.

Specific experience, given the natural immobility of land, is a *centripetal* force tying family members together and contributing to *ex ante* consumption-smoothing. However, the scope for mitigating the effects of adverse weather is limited. What can be done if such actions fail to sustain incomes? Some means by which income shortfalls are made up *ex post* is required. However, by concentrating in one location, the family gives up the gains from spatial diversification, which makes *ex post* consumption-smoothing more difficult. The covariant nature of weather risk and the need to smooth consumption would create an incentive for the family to diversify income sources spatially. Thus there is also a *centrifugal* force tending to spread family members over space, given risk prospects.

While risk considerations increase the returns to the spatial spread of income sources, the costs of coordinating and monitoring a geographically diverse income-pooling scheme also rise with the separation of partners in the scheme. Indeed, it is the positive association between risk-spreading from locational diversity and information and monitoring costs entailed in limiting the scope for cheating that is in part responsible for the absence of crop or income insurance. Can the family sustain an efficient income-pooling scheme across space while minimizing moral hazard and maintaining the gains from experience that are tied to specific plots of land?

Consider first the possibility that the family simply splits, with some members migrating to settle apart from the origin household. The productivity of the new, split-off household would be lower than that of the origin household, as the specific experience returns would be lower on the newly acquired land. Indeed, *ex post* income-pooling considerations would lead to the minimization of the similarity of both land and weather across the two households and thus minimization of the relevance of experience on the family land. An alternative scheme, however, would have one family member transferred into an existing, established household with experience on its own land and income covaring minimally with that of the origin household. In this case, the origin household has an incentive to support the destination household to the extent that the household cares about its former member. Moreover, to the extent that the family member cares about the origin family, the family member will see to it that the destination household does not cheat—the departed family member is like a resident agent of the origin household. Thus, altruism, an important characteristic of families, contributes to the efficiency of spatial income pooling by creating a verification and monitoring capacity.

This latter scheme describes the typical pattern of marriages in rural India, as will be described below. Daughters typically leave the village in which they are born to live with their new husband in his household of birth. Why are daughters and not sons mobile? Given the division of labor in which women contribute less time to agricultural production, there is smaller loss from the reduction in experiential capital upon the migration of a woman compared to a man. Thus, an arrangement in which men are immobile and inherit the family land, and in which there are maritally mobile women establishing ties with spatially spread families, facilitates risk-sharing in the face of covariant risks while maximizing the returns from experience capital (Rosenzweig and Stark 1989).

### *Effects of Technical Change*

One of the most important potential effects of the introduction of technical change is on the returns to human capital. First, under a new technology, past experience becomes less relevant to production decisions. The new regime of best production practices that characterize the new technology obsolesces experience. As a result, it may be expected that one of the ties holding families together, the value of experience specific to the family's land, would erode, with a consequent increase in family breakups and an increase in land sales. In addition, as the value of elders' experience is reduced, such groups may become more vulnerable.

A one-shot change in technology immediately reduces the value of past experience, but if there are no further changes in technology, experiential returns eventually will increase, as farmers become more familiar with the new technology under different varieties of weather and on their own plots of land. Under a regime of constant changes in technology, however, long-term experience never has substantial value and, as hypothesized by T. W. Schultz (1975), the returns to formal schooling rise. This is because under constant change, farmers better able to cope with that change and adapt to new practices earn higher returns. And it is this skill that formal schooling may help to foster. Farmers experiencing a flow of new technologies may need to decode the new information better, for which literacy may be quite useful.

In an environment of *persistent* technical change there is an increase in the rate of return to formal schooling and literacy and a decline in the value of experience. These changes may lead to new family relationships, not only because of the reduced value of specific experience but also because the increase in incomes reduces the need for alternative mechanisms for coping with the vagaries of weather. Farmers are better able to self-insure, and perhaps are less averse to risk, when average incomes are higher. However, informal insurance arrangements involving transfers across households would appear to be inherently fragile. One reason is that beliefs about each farmer's future willingness to participate in the income-pooling arrangement are critical for arrangements undertaken by households that transfer resources to those experiencing negative earnings shocks from those with positive shocks (Foster 1988; Coate and Ravallion 1993). Each participant must believe that other participants will not renege from commitments in the future. These considerations suggest that economic development may have an important effect on the ability and willingness of households to engage in these arrangements.

There are three ways in which economic development, in particular increases in farm earnings brought about by agricultural technological change, may reduce the role of insurance-like transfers and thus the insurance premium attached to marriage. First, technological change may increase mobility; established households will be less likely to remain on the same land due to the erosion of plot-specific experiential returns. As shown by Coate and Ravallion, the prospects of increased mobility of any household participating in the income-pooling scheme increase the divergence between first-best and optimal-constrained transfer arrangements, as the likelihood increases that the future benefits from such a scheme will not be forthcoming to all participants.

A second reason that technical change may reduce the insurance value of marital ties is that increases in earnings, given declining risk aversion and/or improved abilities to accumulate assets, reduce the demand for such insurance. Note that with forward-looking households, it is only necessary that one of the partners believe that future earnings growth will reduce the likelihood of participation for the arrangements to be broken off in the current period. Thus, even farmers who experience earnings growth but who wish to continue such arrangements may not be able to if their partners are less motivated to do so.

Finally, all of the parameters in the risk-sharing decision rules reflect the bargaining parties' mutual assessment of risk and their knowledge of the technology of production. Changes in technology necessitate new arrangements, at least initially, by changing risks and making risk assessment more difficult. This may decrease the ability to risk pool and thus make farmers more reliant on alternative mechanisms to smooth consumption.

In the new environment of technical change and growth, then, the incentives for larger, and vertically extended families with little schooling are reduced. The reduction in returns to experience attenuates the costs of mobility by loosening the ties of generations of kin to the family land, and the decline in the value of family arrangements involving spatial diversification lowers the demand for larger families. Moreover, if the returns to schooling also rise, then in order to mitigate the costs of such schooling, families will reduce the number of children they will have, as elaborated in Becker and Lewis (1973).

## The Data and Empirical Features of the Rural Indian Economy

In order to ascertain if the relationships between family arrangements, human capital, and growth elaborated above are useful depictions of reality, it is important to have data that describe household structures in settings with and without technical change. There are two data sets describing rural India that are quite useful for this purpose. One of these, the International Crop Research Institute for the Semi-Arid Tropics (ICRISAT) Village Studies survey data, provides information on income, expenditures, production resources, assets, and family membership for thirty farmers in ten villages in the semi-arid tropics of India, many of whom were surveyed for as many as ten years. This survey was begun in 1975 in six villages in three agroclimatic regions. In three of those villages, the farmers (and ten households not owning land in each village) were surveyed for ten years, in three others for seven years. In addition, a retrospective questionnaire administered in 1984 elicited retrospective information on marriages, farming experience, and land ownership, which is particularly relevant to the study of the family.

There are two other important features of this data set for an inquiry into the determinants of family-human capital interactions. First, although the data were collected after the green revolution was well under way in India, the semi-arid tropical areas were not directly affected, as the low levels and erratic nature of the rainfall in such areas preclude the use of the new seed varieties of wheat or rice. Thus, the data describe a setting in which there is little technical progress. A second important feature of the data is that there is time-series information on daily rainfall, making it possible to measure an important source of risk and thus study how risk differentially shapes family relationships and the returns to human capital under a technologically stagnant regime.

The longitudinal nature of the ICRISAT data makes it useful for depicting the consumption-smoothing problem confronting farmers. Figure 1 displays the aggregate fluctuations in farm profits from crop production in the original villages for the period 1975–83. As can be seen, the fluctuations are large, and with the exception of two of the villages depicted by the solid lines where there were some improvements in seed varieties (sorghum and cotton) in 1981, trendless. A computation of the intertemporal coefficient of variation (the intertemporal standard deviation divided by the mean) for each of the farmers in these villages indicates that for the average farmer the standard deviation in profits is 25 percent higher than mean profits. To benchmark this figure, I calculated the same statistic based on seven years of annual earnings using U.S. data on white males 25–29 years of age in 1971. For this group, the average coefficient of variation was only 39; earnings variability was thus more than three times higher among farmers in the ICRISAT region than among white males in the United States.

Another important feature indicated by figure 1 is the covariability in incomes. As noted, the villages are grouped into sets of two in three regions. This is depicted in the figure by the use of common line patterns for the groups, and as can be seen the intertemporal movements in aggregate profits are quite closely correlated, particularly in the two solid-line villages, whose distance apart is only 20 kilometers. The data thus suggest that earnings fluctuations and the covariability in earnings are important characteristics of the agricultural environment.[3]

**Figure 1. Profits from Crop Production**

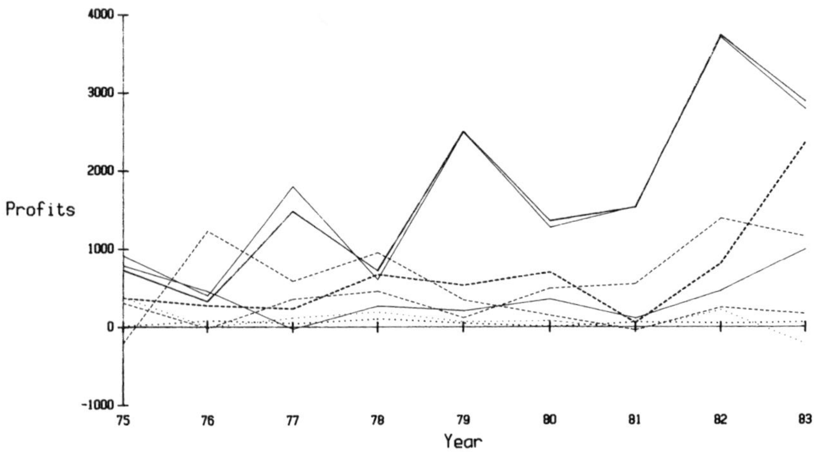


The ICRISAT data cannot be used to assess directly the consequences of technical change. As noted, and as indicated by the ICRISAT data, an important feature of the Indian experience with respect to the introduction of the newer higher-yielding grain varieties in the early 1960s is the spatial variability in the degree to which the green revolution took hold, chiefly because of location-specific heterogeneity in soil and weather conditions. In recognition of the selective potential for the success of the new technologies, the government of India in 1961 implemented a program, the Intensive Agricultural District Program (IADP), in one district in each state in India (two in the state of Kerala) in which it was expected that the improved grain varieties were likely to be particularly productive. The program's objective was to facilitate the adoption of the new inputs and the implementation of new agricultural practices associated with the new inputs—an early example of a governmental program attempting to "pick winners"!

To assess the income distribution consequences of the new grain varieties, the National Council of Applied Economic Research (NCAER) undertook a national survey of rural households in 250 villages in 1968, the Additional Rural Income Survey (ARIS), based on a stratified random sample in which one of the sampling strata was defined by the presence of the IADP program in the district. One-third of the sample thus included households from each of the IADP districts (National Council of Applied Economic Research 1975). Households were interviewed three times annually from the crop year 1968–69 through the crop year 1970–71 resulting in three years of information on a sample of 4,118 households, approximately two-thirds of which were farming households. The sampling scheme of the ARIS survey enables both a more generalizable view of Indian households and behavior and an assessment of the effects of technical change. With the information provided on production, household demography, and income sources taken in the early stages of the green revolution for a national probability sample of rural households, we can assess how typical the six to ten villages in the ICRISAT sample are as well as the consequences, at least initially, of the introduction of continuing agricultural technical progress.

Both data sets reveal a consistent picture of household structure and stability. The NCAER-ARIS data indicate that 62 percent of farm families are characterized by vertical extension (two adult generations of co-resident kin), with only 7.5 percent characterized by horizontal extension (adult siblings co-residing without their parents). The ICRISAT data are similar; they show 70 percent of the farm households vertically extended and only 3 percent horizontally extended. The ICRISAT retrospective data also indicate that households are stable and immobile, with less than 7 percent of household heads born outside of the village in which they were currently living. This stability is also reflected in the rarity of land sales indicated in the NCAER data, with less than 2 percent of farm households having sold any land in the last year of the survey (when this information was elicited). In contrast to the immobility of households and household heads, the women are mobile, as indicated by the ICRISAT retrospective data: 94 percent of the adult *married* women in the sample were born outside of the village in which they were currently residing. These figures on the immobility of men and the mobility of married women in rural areas in the ICRISAT data are echoed in the 1981 Population Census of India, which indicates that 80 percent of all lifetime migrants, persons not residing in the village where they were born, are women.

## Returns to Experience in a Stationary Environment

The patterns of household structure and mobility (and immobility) are broadly consistent with the hypothesis that returns to experience are sufficiently important in stationary but risky agricultural settings to bind the household to the family land, particularly those members who specialize in production. But is the basic assumption correct, that experience has a high return related to coping with the consequences of adverse weather in a stationary economy? To have some confidence in the experience-household structure association, which has important implications for the consequences to families of economic growth, it would be desirable to estimate the returns to experience.

Both the NCAER-ARIS and ICRISAT data sets permit estimation of the returns to farming experience. The NCAER data identify for each of the three years of the survey whether or not there was adverse weather in the village in which the household resides. It is thus possible to estimate the effects of bad weather on farm profits and the way these effects are mitigated, if at all, by farmer experience. Based on regression estimates, figure 2 shows how profits earned under adverse weather conditions are related to the age structure and other characteristics of households, given their average profitability in the years in which weather conditions were normal.[4] Each bar represents the percentage fall in profits from normal or good weather profits resulting from bad weather for households with different characteristics. The first bar on the left represents the percentage shortfall from normal profits (39.7 percent) for households in which the eldest person is less than forty years old and in which there is no extension aid. The next bar represents the profit shortfall in an otherwise identical household in which the eldest person is as old as fifty-nine—the effect of adding a person in the forty to fifty-nine age range to a household in which the eldest is less than forty. The effect is to decrease the shortfall by 10 percentage points. When the eldest is sixty or over, the shortfall declines by an additional 15 percentage points to 15.3 percent (third bar). Thus the presence of an elder over fifty-nine years of age halves the adverse effect of bad weather compared to a household in which the eldest person is less than sixty.

**Figure 2. Percentage Fall in Profits Due to Bad Weather by Family Type**

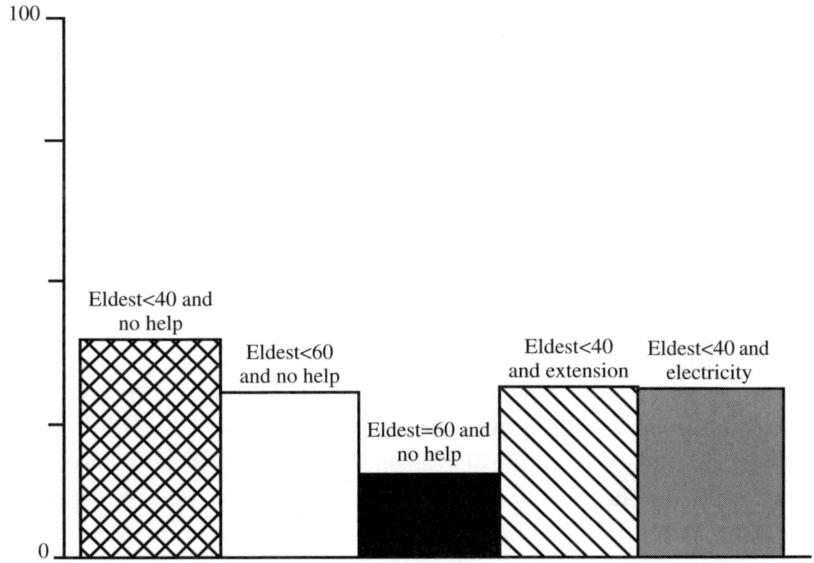


As a benchmark with which to compare the age structure effects, the next bars in the figure represent the profit shortfalls in households like the first, with no elders over forty, but with extension aid and electrification, respectively. These figures indicate that the provision of extension services has a comparable effect on the mitigation of adverse weather to adding an elder between the ages of forty and fifty-nine to the "young" household (the percentage shortfall declines from 39.7 to 31.5 as compared to 30.4), but is only half as effective as adding an elder who is sixty or more years of age. The effect of electrification, which permits irrigation and thus better water control, is similar to the extension service (a fall of 31.0 percent compared to 31.5), and evidently less valuable for limiting the consequences of bad weather than having an individual in the family with forty or more years of farming experience.

The results in figure 2 suggest the importance of farming experience in a stationary environment characterized by erratic rainfall. However, they are not fully satisfactory because (1) age and experience on the family's land are not necessarily the same, although the dearth of land sales suggests that they are highly correlated; and (2) the association between age structure and profits is not necessarily indicative of the effects of age structure, but may instead mean that higher profits in bad weather affect household age structure. Specifically, vertical extension may be a "normal" good—households with higher profits in bad weather may simply prefer to have elders co-reside compared to less fortunate households. Or, for households in which bad weather somehow does not strongly affect profits, the elderly are more likely to survive.

The ICRISAT data permit, in contrast to the NCAER data, a more exact reconstruction of each farmer's experience on the family's land, based on the retrospective questionnaire providing a complete plot-specific history for all owned plots of land for all heads of households. Moreover, the extended number of years over which the farmers are observed permits better controls for unobserved factors that may affect profits and thus the family age structure. Based on the restrospective questionnaire on plot ownership and cultivation administered to all sample households, the total experience of each household head on all owned plots of land, differentiated by whether the land was irrigated or not, was computed for each of the ten years of the sample survey. For each household in each year, cumulative experience on owned plots for each type of land (dry or irrigated) was computed as the weighted average, by plot size, of the total years that each plot (whether owned or not) had been cultivated by the household head. One can then examine how the change in the real value of net profits from cultivation is related to the changes in (1) total experience on each type of land, (2) total holdings of each land type, (3) rainfall in the year (rain per day in three of the most critical months during the rainy season, July, August, and September), and (4) rainfall interacted with both land owned and experience. By looking at the association between the change in profits and the changes in the determinants of profits, the influence on profits of permanent but unmeasured characteristics of the farm households, such as ability or healthiness, which may also affect the number of accumulated years of cultivation, are eliminated.

Figure 3 reports in graphical form the relationships between farm profits and rainfall for the farmers surveyed by ICRISAT classified into three experience groups: those with ten, twenty, and thirty years of farmer experience on their own plots of land.[5] The figures show that, among farmers with the same schooling, with the same irrigated and dry landholdings, and who are the same age, increases in specific experience contribute significantly to increased agricultural profits.[6] At the sample mean rainfall (5 mm per day), it can be seen that farmers with thirty years of specific experience (3,963 rupees) have significantly higher profits than those with twenty years of experience (2,596 rupees) and ten years (1,459 rupees). Moreover, and consistent with the results from the NCAER-ARIS sample, the sensitivity of profits to rainfall is also less for the more experienced farmers—the relationship between profits and rainfall is less steep for the more experienced farmers compared to those farmers with less experience. Indeed, at the lowest level of rainfall, 2 mm, the ratio of profits for the most experienced farmers to those with the least experience is 4.5 to 1, while at the highest levels of rainfall the ratio is only 1.8 to 1 as a consequence of the differential sensitivities of profitability to rainfall across the experience groups.

The results reported in figure 3 thus indicate that there are significant gains from the experience accumulated by farmers from the continuous cultivation of land in the environment of the ICRISAT villages where technical change is not a significant factor. The magnitudes of the effects are such as to make it profitable for families to try to hold on to their landholdings, and for cultivating members of the household to stay on the family land. Moreover, the data also indicate, although these results are not shown, that the schooling level of the farmers played no role in either altering the effects of rainfall on profits or in determining the level of profits. Where there are few or no innovations to learn about, the skills provided by formal schooling are evidently not profitable.

**Figure 3. Relationship of Farm Profits to Rainfall, by Farmer Experience**

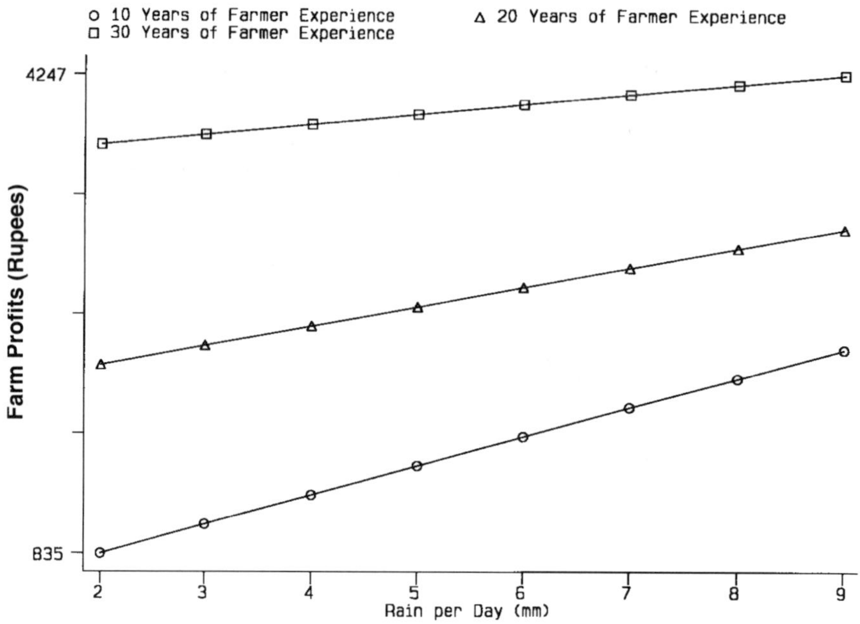


## Risk-Diversification Gains from Marital Mobility

While figures 2 and 3 suggest that specific experience in farming can alleviate some of the adverse consequences for earnings due to shortfalls in rainfall, they also indicate that farm profits are sensitive to rainfall variability even among the most experienced farmers. Farm households thus still need mechanisms to smooth their consumption in the face of *ex post* earnings fluctuations. As discussed earlier, having family members who reside some distance from the household can potentially contribute to consumption-smoothing by pooling earnings from spatially diversified income sources. If there is such pooling, then transfers of income should be observed to originate from outside the villages of the households and not from nearby neighbors and in particular from the destination households of married daughters and the origin households of the wives of the men in the household. The ICRISAT data provide information on the approximate location of transaction partners for many of the transactions undertaken by the surveyed households, which can be used to ascertain if transfers are locally based.

Table 1 compares the origin, by location, for three types of income for the three ICRISAT villages with the longest time-series of information on transactions (ten years). These numbers indicate that the likelihood of a transaction originating outside of the village is three times higher for a transfer than for crop sale and a transfer is four times more likely to originate outside the village than is the sale of labor services. Moreover, among transactions with partners residing outside the village, income transfers originate the farthest from the village—three times farther than the external purchasers of crops and almost four times farther than the employers of labor.

**Table 1. Location of Origin of Income, by Type, in Three ICRISAT Villages**

| Income type | Total number of transactions | Value share from outside of village | Mean distance to source (kilometers) |
|---|---|---|---|
| Transfers | 3,000 | 58.7 | 24.9 |
| Daily labor | 10,940 | 24.8 | 6.5 |
| Sale of crops | 13,083 | 19.0 | 8.3 |

SOURCE: Rosenzweig (1988b).

Although there is no information in the ICRISAT data on the identity of transaction partners, the issue can be addressed indirectly. One way to do this is to ask whether households who are more successful in smoothing consumption are those with a greater number of marital "connections," as indicated by the number of married women in the household. If such marriage-based income-pooling schemes are important, then one should observe that adding married women to the household reduces consumption variability. Information on annual consumption is available for each household and can be used to compute, over a ten-year period, the variability in consumption for each household. Similarly, based on annual profit information, a measure of household-specific profit variability can also be constructed.

If households can perfectly smooth their consumption, then there should be no relationship between the variability in earnings or profits that they experience and the variability in their consumption. On the other hand, if households cannot smooth at all, consumption variability will be identical to earnings variability. Figure 4 charts the extent to which actual consumption variability deviates from perfect consumption-smoothing (no variability) for households classified by the number of married women in them and by their inherited wealth.[7] The figure shows that households least successful in smoothing consumption *ex post* have the highest deviations and the tallest bars.

**Figure 4. Percent Deviation from Perfect Consumption-Smoothing**

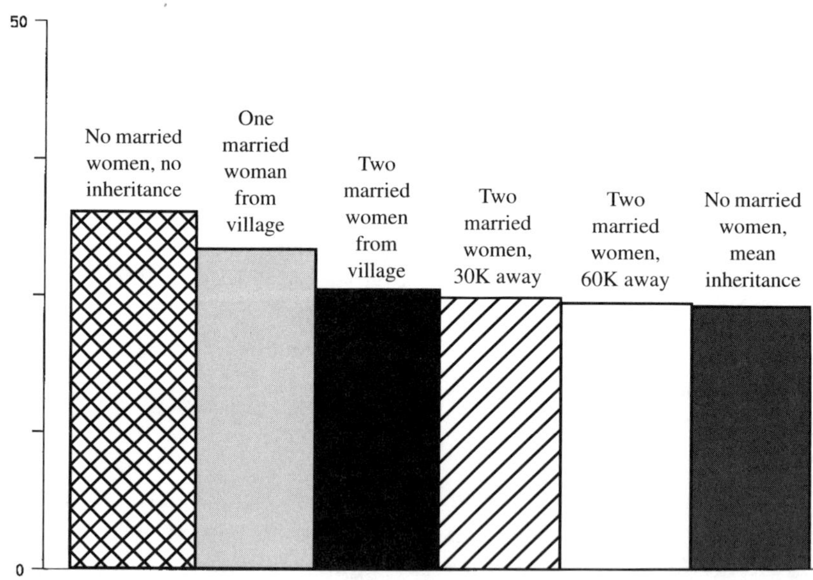


The first bar on the left depicts the shortfall from perfect *ex post* consumption-smoothing for a household with no married women and no inherited wealth; for this household, approximately 68 percent of profit variability is carried over into consumption variability so that the household's consumption variance deviates from perfect consumption-smoothing by 32 percent. The next two bars represent the extent of consumption-smoothing for otherwise identical households, in terms of landholdings, total number of adult males and females, and levels of schooling, but with one and two (resident) married women who came from a household located in the village, respectively. These households, as can be seen, experience less consumption variability than the first household with no married women, by about 7 percentage points for the household with two married women.

The next two bars show what would happen in a household with two married women if the average distance of the origin household from the village of the respondent household was to increase to 30 and 60 kilometers, respectively. As can be seen, increasing the distance between households does also reduce consumption variability, although the effects are smaller than the creation of household ties via marriage as represented by the presence of married women.

Finally, the last bar shows the extent to which the addition of capital to a household with no married women also reduces the impact of earnings variability on consumption variability. In this case, it is the effect of providing the sample mean inheritance of 79,000 (1984) rupees, or about $4,000, to the household with neither wealth nor married women. The height of this bar indicates that this amount of wealth, coincidentally, has almost the exact same impact of the degree of *ex post* consumption-smoothing as does having two married women in the household with origin families located 60 kilometers away. In terms of improving a household's ability to smooth consumption in the face of earnings variability, these married women are equivalent in value to having an inheritance of 79,00 rupees! This last "experiment" also demonstrates that increased wealth, which is one consequence of economic growth, is a substitute for the informal risk-pooling scheme associated with marriage.

## Consequences of Agricultural Technical Change for Schooling Investments and Household Stability

I turn now to the evidence on how technical change affects the returns to schooling and family stability exploiting the geographically selective nature of the green revolution in India and, in particular, the identification by the Indian government of specific districts in which such technology would yield the greatest productivity gains, the IADP districts. How successful was the Indian government in identifying where growth would be most rapid? In this case, the areas selected do appear to have grown more rapidly than did other areas as a whole. Figure 5 plots the ratios of indices of aggregate output to 1960 levels in IADP and non–IADP areas from 1960 up to the survey date.[8] As can be seen prior to 1967, output movements in both IADP and non–IADP districts were similarly affected by weather variation and did not exhibit growth. After 1966, however, output grew at a higher rate in the IADP areas and the similarity in movements is attenuated, reflecting in part the different agricultural technologies being used. Moreover, adoption rates of the new high-yielding grain varieties in IADP areas were significantly higher than elsewhere as of 1970–71 and real agricultural wage rates in the decade between 1961 and 1971 rose by 24 percent in IADP areas compared to 6.4 percent in non–IADP areas (Rosenzweig 1990). Thus, the IADP areas were, at least up to the time of the survey, experiencing higher rates of growth in earnings after the onset of the green revolution.

**Figure 5. Ratio of Aggregate Output to 1960 Output in IADP and Non-IADP Districts**

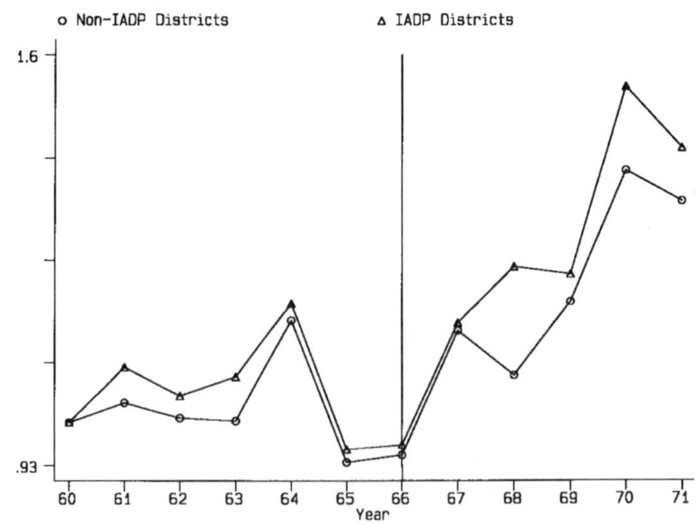

It is, of course, not possible to know on the basis of the 1968–71 NCAER-ARIS data, collected approximately eight years after the introduction of higher-yielding seeds, whether the returns to schooling rose more in districts where farmers directly benefited from the new technologies, because we only have cross-sectional evidence. The evidence does suggest that rates of return to primary schooling in 1970–71 were higher in the IADP areas, but they may also have been higher in 1950 or 1960 as well (Rosenzweig 1990).

On the basis of school enrollment data for children and schooling attainment information for adults in the 1970–71 survey, however, a retrospective history of schooling investments can be reconstructed. It is thus possible to ascertain if schooling investments rose more in the IADP districts since the onset of the green revolution compared to non–IADP districts. By comparing the pre- and post-green revolution schooling investment rates in the IADP and non–IADP districts, aggregate trends in schooling over the 1961–71 period are effectively "controlled for." This intertemporal comparison from the cross-sectional survey data can be accomplished based on the fact that members of households aged twenty-five and above in 1971 who attended primary school would have completed their primary schooling prior to the introduction of the new high-yielding grain varieties, while those persons aged ten to fourteen in 1971 who attended primary school would have completed their primary school education after the green revolution began.

Figure 6 shows the changes in the percentage of male illiteracy in farm households in the non–IADP areas and in the IADP districts before and after the beginning of the green revolution. The figure shows that male illiteracy was lower in the IADP districts *before* the new technologies were introduced. This pre-1961 difference in literacy could not therefore have been caused by the growth induced by the subsequent availability of the new grain varieties. However, the figure also reveals that the proportion of men who were illiterate fell more after the new technologies were first introduced in the IADP areas compared to the non–IADP areas, which experienced considerably less growth: the proportion of men who were illiterate in farm households decreased by 14.5 percentage points, a 56 percent drop, in IADP districts, and by 12.1 percentage points, a 30 percent drop, in non–IADP districts. The cohort data thus indicate that increases in the pace of development, fueled by exogenous technical change, lead to increases in human capital investment, consistent with the hypothesis that technology growth raises the returns to schooling.

**Figure 6. Male Illiteracy in Non–IADP and IADP Districts: 1961 and 1971**

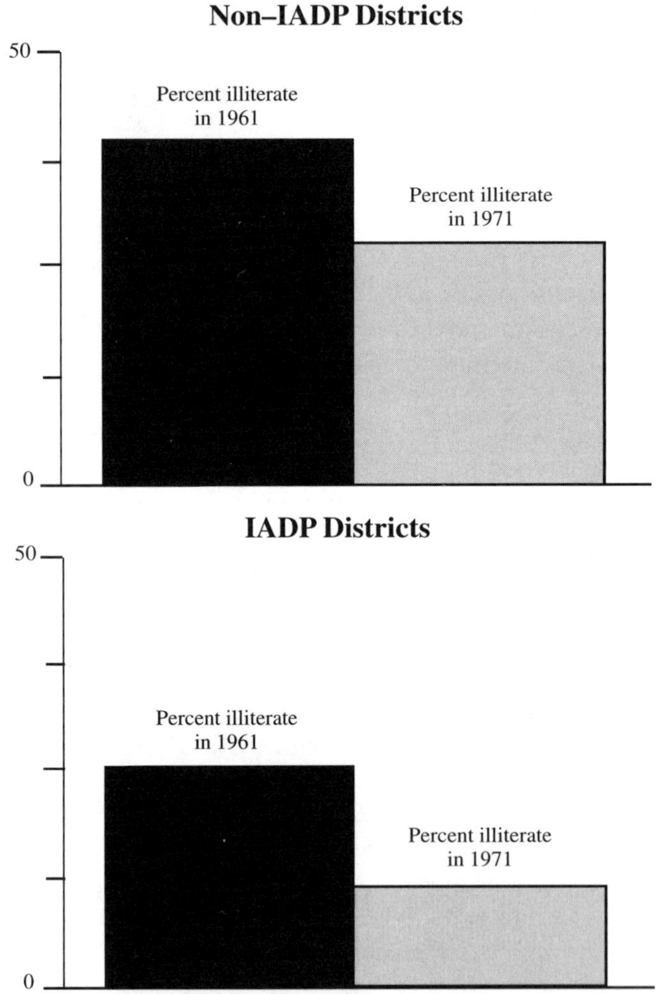


It is also possible to compare the pre- and post-green revolution cumulative fertility experiences of comparably aged women in the

IADP and non–IADP districts using a similar cohort analysis based on the retrospective fertility rosters of the married women in 1970–71 to see if families were getting smaller as a consequence of technical change. The children born to women aged twenty-five to thirty-four in 1971 in IADP districts should almost wholly reflect the green revolution experience, while the cumulative fertility of women aged twenty-five to thirty-four residing in IADP districts in 1961 and that of women aged twenty-five to thirty-four residing in non–IADP districts in either 1961 or 1971 should not have been directly influenced by the new technologies. Figure 7 plots the cumulative fertility (children ever born) of women aged twenty-five to thirty-four in the IADP and non–IADP districts for the years 1961 and 1971. The figure suggests that there were substantial effects on fertility associated with the introduction of technical change. While cumulative fertility was higher by almost one-third of a child in the IADP districts compared to the non–IADP areas in 1961, the cumulative fertility rates fell by much more over the subsequent decade in the IADP districts—from 3.44 children to 3.04 children in the IADP districts compared to a fall from 3.11 to 3.03 children in the rest of India. By the end of the 1960s, fertility in the IADP and non–IADP areas was virtually the same.

**Figure 7. 1961–71 Change in Fertility: Women 25–34 in IADP and Non–IADP Areas**

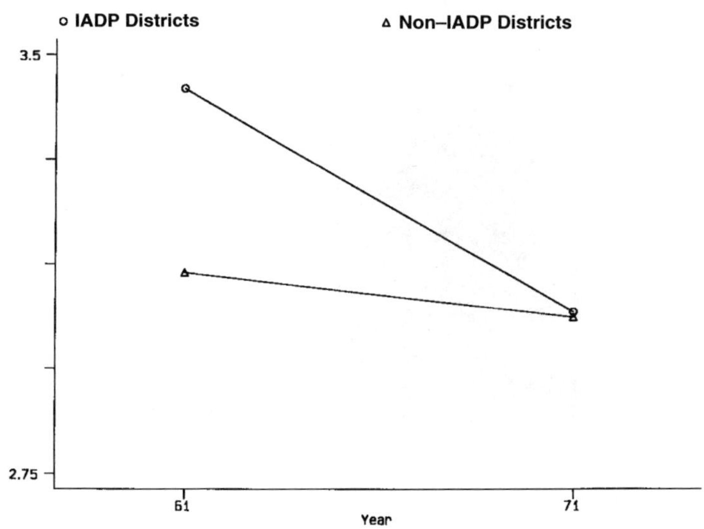

Do the declines in fertility reflect the reduced return to larger families from risk-spreading and the reduced stability of households? The evidence based on the 1968–71 NCAER-ARIS data suggests that households in the IADP districts were significantly less likely to receive a financial transfer than households in non–IADP districts experiencing the same shortfalls in income and with the same household structure. However, again, the lower efficacy of income-pooling in the IADP districts observed in 1968–71 may have existed before the onset of the green revolution; before and after evidence is needed.

Two new findings on the *change* in the stability of landholdings and in family structure are associated with the introduction of new grain varieties. First, as noted, new varieties of two principal crops, sorghum and cotton, were introduced in two of the ICRISAT villages in 1981. Prior to that year, over the 1975–1980 period, 4.8 percent of households sold land in a typical year. After 1981, based on information in the years 1982–84, 6.3 percent of households sold their holdings. This increase in land divestment is consistent with the erosion of the returns from specific experience associated with new technologies.

**Figure 8. Proportion of Households Splitting in Non–IADP and IADP Districts, 1971–1982**

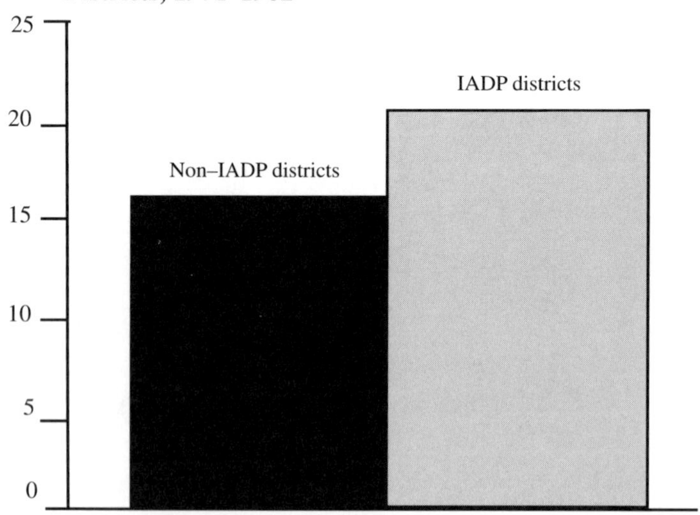

A second and more important piece of evidence is from a preliminary look at newly available data from a 1982 follow-up survey undertaken by NCAER, which reinterviewed a subset of the original 1970–71 NCAER–ARIS households. By matching the two surveys for households in which the head was still alive in 1982, it is possible to discern which households split over the 1971–82 period, where a "split" household is defined as one in which an adult male has left permanently. The results of this preliminary matching, performed jointly with Prem Vashishtha of NCAER, are shown in figure 8. It indicates that in the non–IADP districts, the proportion of households that split was 29 percent less than the proportion who split in the IADP districts subsequent to the initial survey in 1970–71— 16.8 percent of households split by 1982 in the non–IADP districts compared to 21.6 in the IADP districts. These differences in the probability of break-up were not due to either differences in initial wealth across the two areas, as indicated by landholdings in 1970–71, or to differences in the schooling attainment of heads in 1970–71, as the results are unaffected by controlling for these household characteristics.

## Conclusion

In this essay I have briefly discussed some of the connections between economic development, the family, and the returns to human capital. The evidence from the Indian experience, in which economic growth in the rural sector was propelled by exogenous technical change starting in the mid-1960s, appears to suggest that a fuller understanding of changing family arrangements and family values cannot be achieved without attention to the economic problem of security facing households and to the effects of economic growth on the relative rates of return to formal schooling and experience. An examination of Indian data soon after the beginning of the revolutionary transformation of agriculture, from a relatively stable, tradition-based regime to one which is dynamic, suggests that technical change can have important destabilizing effects on basic institutions such as the the family by reducing the returns to experience and by making risk-spreading arrangements among family members more difficult in an environment of increased uncertainty.

There are some general implications for policy from these findings. First, it is notable that the significant decline in fertility in the growth areas relative to the rest of India occurred without direct governmental intervention. Public family planning efforts were not targeted to those areas. When lower fertility is a public goal, such efforts are not always necessary if economic growth is significant. On the other hand, the demand for services that a family planning program would provide was evidently higher in the high-growth areas. Moreover, the less substantial relative increase in schooling may in part reflect a lack of response in terms of school facilities. Given the Indian government's prescience in selecting areas of potential growth, it would appear that an anticipatory reallocation of public resources aimed at facilitating schooling, fertility reduction, and, perhaps, increasing income security would have been desirable. Indeed, it is hoped that the further study of the consequences of economic growth for family relationships and for human capital investments will provide a more effective basis for formulating policies that will mitigate some of the problems associated with adapting to the new, and less stable, circumstances a high-growth regime entails.

## NOTES

1. See Rosenzweig and Binswanger (1993) and Rosenzweig and Wolpin (1993) for studies of how weather risk alters the allocation of productive durables in Indian farming and the consequences of different production portfolios.

2. The intergenerational gains from specific experience are more formally modeled in Rosenzweig and Wolpin (1985).

3. The relationships between the distance between the ICRISAT villages and the intervillage correlations in rainfall and farm profits are positive and statistically significant (Rosenzweig 1988b).

4. Only households experiencing at least one good-weather year were selected for this analysis. In the crop year 1968–69, 59 percent of households were in a village that experienced adverse weather; the percentages for the subsequent two crop years were 27 and 14 percent, respectively. For details, see Rosenzweig and Wolpin (1985).

5. For details on the estimates underlying the figure, see Rosenzweig (1988a).

6. The figures are computed for farmers at age fifty, with otherwise average schooling and landholdings in the sample.

7. The estimation procedures used to obtain the results in the figure are described in Rosenzweig and Stark (1989).

8. The construction of the output series for the districts included in the NCAER-ARIS survey is described in Binswanger, Khandker, and Rosenzweig (1993).

## References

Becker, Gary S., and H. Gregg Lewis. 1973. "On the Interaction between the Quantity and Quality of Children," *Journal of Political Economy* 81 (March/April): S279–88.

Binswanger, Hans P., S.R. Khandker, and Mark R. Rosenzweig. 1993. "How Infrastructure and Financial Institutions Affect Agricultural Investment Output and Investment in India," *Journal of Development Economics* 41, 2: 337–366.

Binswanger, Hans P., and Mark R. Rosenzweig. 1986. "Behavioral and Material Determinants of Production Relations in Agriculture," *Journal of Development Studies* 22, 3 (April): 503–539.

Coate, Stephen, and Martin Ravallion. 1993. "Reciprocity without Commitment: Characterization and Performance of Informal Insurance Arrangements," *Journal of Development Economics* 40, 1 (February): 1–24.

Foster, Andrew D. 1988. "Why Things Fall Apart: A Strategic Analysis of Repeated Interaction in Rural Financial Markets." Mimeo, University of California, Berkeley.

National Council of Applied Economic Research. 1975. *Changes in Rural Income in India, 1968–69, 1969–70, 1970–71.* New Delhi: NCAER.

Rosenzweig, Mark R. 1988a. "Risk, Private Information and the Family." Papers and Proceedings, *American Economic Review* (May): 245–250.

_____. 1988b. "Risk, Implicit Contracts and the Family in Rural Areas of Low-Income Countries," *Economic Journal* (December): 1148–1170.

_____. 1990. "Population Growth and Human Capital Investments: Theory and Evidence," *Journal of Political Economy* 98, 5, Part 2 (October): 538–570.

_____. 1993. "Women, Insurance Capital, and Economic Development in Rural India," *Journal of Human Resources* 28, 4: 735–758.

Rosenzweig, Mark R., and Hans P. Binswanger. 1993. "Wealth, Weather Risk and the Composition and Profitability of Agricultural Investments," *Economic Journal* 103 (January): 56–78.

Rosenzweig, Mark R., and Oded Stark. 1989. "Consumption-Smoothing, Migration and Marriage: Evidence from Rural India," *Journal of Political Economy* 59, 4 (August): 905–926.

Rosenzweig, Mark R., and Kenneth I. Wolpin. 1985. "Specific Experience, Household Structure and Intergenerational Transfers: Farm Family Land and Labor Arrangements in Developing Countries," *Quarterly Journal of Economics* Supplement C, 402: 961–987.

_____. 1993. "Credit Market Constraints and the Accumulation of Durable Production Assets in Low-Income Countries: Investments in Bullocks," *Journal of Political Economy* 101, 2: 223–244.

Schultz, Theodore W. 1975. "The Value of the Ability to Deal with Disequilibria," *Journal of Economic Literature* 13 (September): 827–46.

# Can the U.S. System of Workplace Training Survive Global Competition?

Peter B. Doeringer
*Boston University*

One of the most well-documented facts of modern labor economics is that education and training, or what economists call human capital investments, have high payoff in terms of income and productivity (Denison 1985). In a country like the United States with a large public education system and high levels of college attendance, estimates are that investments in schooling yield a rate of return in excess of 10 percent and that over half of all national wealth is in the form of the education and skills of the labor force (U.S. Congress 1973).

Increases in human capital have traditionally translated into rising productivity and growth in earnings (Denison 1985; Jorgenson 1988). During the postwar period, the American economy could regularly count on productivity increases of around 3 percent a year. After the OPEC oil shock of 1973, however, this rate plummeted to nine-tenths of a percent.

Many explanations have been offered to explain this decline—falling R&D expenditures, low rates of savings and investment, increased governmental regulation, and even the bureaucratic and myopic behavior of managers (Griliches 1988; Jorgenson 1988; Olson 1988). However, a series of blue-ribbon competitiveness commissions advanced the thesis that the accumulating weaknesses of American schools were also a significant drag on productivity growth.

The Commission on Workforce Quality and Labor Market Efficiency (1989) reported that "vast numbers of American students cannot meet the educational requirements of today's workplace, much less those of the next century...." A study by the American Society of Training Directors (1989) concluded that the problem of "deficiencies in basic workplace skills is a growing one... [which is] driving the nation toward a human capital deficit...that threatens the competitiveness of economic institutions...." A *Business Week* (1988) cover story on human capital reported that "the U.S. has lost much ground to competitors, and investing in people looks like the way to retake it." The general conclusion of this wave of reports was that educational reform and new partnerships between education and business were needed to restore productivity growth and to make American industry competitive.

## The U.S. System of Workplace Training and Productivity

While not wishing to diminish the importance of education reform, I would argue that the crux of the nation's human capital deficiencies does not lie exclusively in its schools, and that improvements in education are not as central to solving the nation's productivity and human capital problems as many have argued. Even if schooling could be a critical part of the long-term solution to the nation's competitiveness problems, it could do little to rebuild the productive capacity of today's workers who are already out of school and who will account for two-thirds of the next decade's labor force. Instead, the problem is rooted in the weakening of America's *workplace* system for building labor productivity—where I define productivity to include effort, commitment, and problem-solving capacity, as well as job skills.

Schools in this country have never contributed much to this broad conception of productivity and are unlikely ever to play a major role, given the organization of work in American industry. The K–12 school system, and even vocational and technical schools and higher education, are largely intended to provide a once-in-a-lifetime foundation of basic skills for young workers who are entering the labor market. No matter how high the quality, common denominator training in foundation skills for entry-level jobs cannot prepare workers to operate specific technologies, to accommodate quickly to changing products and materials, to meet rising standards of quality, or to solve day-to-day production problems. Nor can it prepare workers for the inevitable changes in skills that will occur during their working lives.

Lifetime skills of this sort can only be learned through experience gained on-the-job by working on the shop floor or in other work settings. A sense of the importance of such workplace training can be obtained by comparing the earnings of recent school graduates who have little or no work experience with those of workers whose productivity has been increased through experiential learning. The earnings of full-time, male high school graduates, for example, will about double after thirty years of work experience and a similar amount of work experience will more than double the earnings of college graduates.

If I have persuaded you that the "workplace training system" is worthy of attention as a source of improved earnings and productivity, then it is important to understand how this system works and what has been happening to it in recent years. I will use the example of production workers in manufacturing as an illustration, but many of the same principles apply more generally to other occupations and other sectors.

## Recent Trends in the Workplace Training System

The United States actually has two systems of workplace training. One is what my radical colleagues call the "Taylorist" or "Fordist" system that originated in mass production manufacturing in the early part of the twentieth century; the second is a newer "high-commitment" system that was initially introduced in nonunion, high-technology manufacturing after World War II.

### *The Fordist System*

Under the Fordist system, workers are hired into entry-level jobs that require little or no skill. Those who pass a probationary period of employment are gradually promoted up the rungs of a job ladder to positions of increasing skill, responsibility, and pay. Promotion generally follows seniority, and each promotion requires additional on-the-job training to bring employees up to full productive capacity.

Many of the skills acquired in this way are unique to a particular company's technology and work organization, and workers therefore acquire human capital that is valuable only in a specific employment situation. The cost to the firm of providing such skills gives employers an incentive to retain trained workers.

At the same time, the lack of transferable skills and the importance of seniority in job ladder promotions mean that if workers quit their jobs to work for another employer, they are likely to lose income because they will have to start again at the bottom of the job ladder. Since changing jobs is costly to both employers and workers, one of the benefits of working under the Fordist system is that senior workers who have acquired the greatest training and experience tend to accumulate the most job security and are the least likely to quit.

The Fordist system, however, is about more than building workforce productivity through on-the-job training and experience. It also involves raising productivity through "effort bargains," often reached collectively between labor and management. Collective bargaining agreements can be seen as "grand" effort bargains that commit workers to a certain work pace in exchange for agreed-upon rates of pay and other conditions of employment. These "grand bargains" are further elaborated through numerous informal "shop floor effort bargains" in which workers supply the extra effort and assistance needed to resolve unanticipated production problems in exchange for time off or other considerations that can be granted by foremen (Kaboolian 1990).

Such collective effort bargains provide a means of ensuring that productivity increases do not unduly threaten job security and that gains in output are shared between labor and management. At the same time, they secure worker consent to providing the regular increases in efficiency that are needed to sustain economic gains and job security over the longer term.

### *The High-Commitment System*

The high-commitment system shares many of the underlying sources of productivity found in the Fordist model. Workers are hired into entry-level jobs and are then promoted to positions of increasing skill, responsibility, and pay.

Where these two systems part company, however, is in the nature of their effort bargains. The high-commitment systems emphasizes *individual,* rather than *collective,* effort bargains. In contrast to the Fordist model which relies on collective bargaining processes to set and enforce the rate of productivity growth, the high-commitment model relies on a complex set of psychological and sociological management techniques to encourage individual workers to internalize the goals and objectives of the company and to act so as to achieve these goals.

Under these individual effort bargains, workers are asked to adopt performance goals and are trained to self-monitor and self-discipline their performance. As soon as a given performance goal is achieved, workers are encouraged to adopt a new effort bargain that incorporates higher production targets.

The *quid pro quo* for these high-commitment effort bargains is the pledge by the company to provide intensive career training and development within the company, fair levels of compensation, and often an implicit guarantee of lifetime employment. The result is continuous improvement in both productivity and career earnings.

### *Comparing the Models*

Both the Fordist and high-commitment systems have in common the ability to enhance labor productivity through workplace training and through the setting of workplace norms that control effort. However, these systems gain productivity at the cost of both high wages and a certain amount of inflexibility that comes from routine adherence to job ladder assignments and from the provision of long-term employment security.

Fordist firms, for example, tend to pay high wages as part of their collective effort bargains, while high-commitment firms typically match or exceed Fordist wage rates as a way of underscoring the fairness of the terms of their effort bargains with individual workers. These high performance pay premiums are not trivial. In high-performance industries such as chemicals and petroleum, nonelectrical machinery (including computers), and primary metals, they range from 16 percent to 29 percent above economywide averages for comparable skills (Katz and Summers 1989).

In economics terms, these productivity-enhancing practices correspond to a concept know as "efficiency wage theory." Efficiency wage theory is a metaphor about how employment relationships can suffer from what economists call "principal-agent" problems because employers (who are the principals) and workers (who are the agents of the employer) have somewhat divergent and adversarial interests that can lead to low labor productivity unless workers' abilities can be precisely measured and workers' productivity closely supervised. Mainstream labor economics has focused on high wage premiums as the motivating force for ensuring that productivity will be maintained, but it has not fully appreciated that wages are only a part of more complex workplace systems that raise productivity through various types of effort bargaining.

### *Employment-At-Will and the Secondary Labor Market*

High-performance, efficiency wage systems contrast sharply with a third, and very different, workplace system that I refer to as "employment-at-will." The employment-at-will system resembles a "spot" market for labor, in which wages and employment are determined by the invisible hand of competition. In the employment-at-will system, jobs are dead end; employers provide little or no training and advancement opportunity; there are no effort bargains or incentive wage premiums above market levels; and employment is impermanent.

Collectively, these jobs belong to the secondary labor market of marginal firms and marginal industries such as clothing and textiles. During much of the postwar period, economists assumed that these low-wage, low-performance industries would gradually be replaced by Fordist and high-commitment industries, thereby further aiding growth in productivity and earnings.

## The Collapse of High-Performance Employment Systems

This assumption has been shattered by sharp declines in the fortunes of high-performance manufacturing plants since the mid-1970s. Profits fell during the 1970s and early 1980s by about one-third from the levels of the 1960s under the pressures of deregulation and loss of market share to international competitors. These pressures rippled through the labor market as over three-fourths of all large manufacturing companies closed or significantly downsized a facility (Berenbeim 1986), causing as many as two million workers a year to be displaced from their jobs.

Employment losses were most severe in import-sensitive industries such as steel and apparel. Employment in basic steel has fallen by 58 percent since 1973, and other mature industries have experienced substantial job cuts—textile employment has fallen by 32 percent and apparel by 29 percent, while the auto industry has lost 16 percent of its jobs. As many as one in five of today's unemployed workers have now permanently lost their jobs (Doeringer et al. 1991, ch. 3).

While some workers have found replacement jobs quickly, displacement for most means being out of work for an average of nine months to a year. Not only are replacement jobs harder to find, but they are also likely to be less permanent and to pay less than the career jobs that they replace (Doeringer et al. 1991, ch. 3).

Reemployment has meant wage losses of 25 percent or more for a quarter to a third of all displaced workers. The biggest losers have been high-seniority workers who have held jobs in high-performance firms (Doeringer et al. 1991, ch. 3). These jobs are also less secure because newly hired workers have the least seniority and because the mix of available jobs is becoming less stable. For example, involuntary part-time employment rose by almost three-fourths between 1973 and 1991 (Mishel and Bernstein 1993, table 4.10), and employment in the temporary help industry exploded during this period (Mishel and Bernstein 1993, tables 4.21 and 4.22; Christensen 1989). These impermanent jobs do not offer the kinds of training opportunities or effort bargains that are available to permanent workers in high-performance firms.

The real earnings of those who remain employed in manufacturing have experienced a similar shock. Prior to the 1970s, real hourly earnings in manufacturing rose at an annual rate of about 1.5 percent. Between 1973 and 1979, however, real hourly earnings in manufacturing rose at about half that rate and actually fell between 1980 and 1988. Overall, real earnings in manufacturing have fallen by over 9 percent since 1979.

Young workers have been hardest hit by these changes. Prior to the 1970s, young males could expect strong gains in real earnings during their twenties as they moved from relatively short-term "youth" jobs to higher-paying and more stable "career" jobs. The restructuring of manufacturing has changed this pattern, leaving a generation of young adults increasingly stranded in low-wage, dead-end, and often part-time service jobs. As a result, the real incomes of young male high school graduates fell by 24 percent between 1973 and 1986, and by 37 percent for high school dropouts (Doeringer et al. 1991, ch. 2).

For those at mid-career, job attachment is becoming less secure as the risk of displacement rises, and even older workers are finding that their once secure career jobs are ending prematurely. Rather than holding a career job until retirement, one in three male workers over fifty-five are moving from career jobs to lower-paid "bridge" jobs. One-fourth of these bridge jobs involve a change of both occupation and industry and half result in a drop in earnings of 25 percent or more (Doeringer et al. 1991, ch. 3; Ruhm 1992).

The degree and persistence of job and earnings losses is unprecedented since the Great Depression of the 1930s; all workers are now at risk of job loss at some point in their careers. While the effects of business restructuring have been most acute for minorities and those with educational disadvantages, even college graduates have been affected. Estimates are that one in five college graduates are now underutilized because they are working in jobs that do not require college degrees—a rate that has almost doubled since 1970 (Hecker 1992).

To some economists, these developments are not a major source of concern. They see such adjustments as evidence that labor in the U.S. economy had become overpriced, overeducated, and inefficiently utilized by world standards. Trimming employment and cutting real wages are the recommended prescriptions for such a situation, and these steps should help to restore the economy to its long-term growth path.

Such an assessment, however, ignores the way in which the nation's workplace training and productivity capacity is also being eroded by industrial restructuring. Much of the reduction in employment and earnings in manufacturing is, in fact, symptomatic of the reconfiguration that is occurring in workplace training systems, and these changes may adversely affect the long-term patterns of productivity and growth in the American economy.

## Breaking Effort Bargains

Employment reductions in large enterprises have obviously diminished the number of workers receiving training and premium pay in high-performance workplaces. However, an even more significant consequence of restructuring is that companies are being forced to reconsider the collective and individual effort bargains that have been one of the lynchpins of productivity improvement in the postwar period.

### *Cutting Wages*

In Fordist workplaces, the grand effort bargains are being changed through wage rollbacks and concessions in other wage entitlements such as cost-of-living allowances (Bell 1989). Shop floor effort bargains are also being broken as centralized bargaining in industries such as steel and autos is being replaced by decentralized and fragmented bargaining that allows for additional local wage reductions (Katz 1992). At the same time, effort bargains are also becoming more uncertain through the introduction of two-tier wage systems, lump-sum and bonus payments, and profit-sharing schemes (Bell 1989).

There has been a similar reneging on effort bargains in high-commitment firms. Pay increases and career advancement have become much less certain, and the implicit guarantees of lifetime employment are being routinely broken by waves of layoffs, sometimes thinly disguised as early retirement programs. Even IBM—the leading proponent of high-commitment effort bargains—has been forced to abandon its long tradition of virtual job guarantees and has begun to rely on layoffs to trim its workforce.

### *Getting More Productivity*

Both Fordist and high-commitment firms are also trying to increase the productivity side of effort bargains. Quality circles and other forms of employee involvement have been adopted to improve productivity, solve quality problems, and more generally to motivate employees to contribute more to business performance (Cole 1989; Kochan, Katz, and McKersie 1986). Concerns with lagging productivity in steel in the 1970s, for example, led to the establishment of plant-level labor-management committees to find ways to increase productivity. More recently, shop floor labor-management committees have been used to address similar problems in autos.

Inflexible work rules and job assignment practices are often identified by management as a major source of labor inefficiency (Kochan, Katz, and McKersie 1986). Such inflexibility is now being combated by consolidating job classifications and by deploying workers more widely within the enterprise. Flexibility in work assignments has also been used to increase the skill and responsibility of production jobs by blurring the dividing line between supervisory and production work.

Decentralization of personnel and labor relations decisions is also seen as a move that will increase labor efficiency by making it easier to change local effort bargains. For example, in a significant break with past practice, individual auto plants and union locals have been allowed to negotiate explicit labor cost reductions to forestall subcontracting and have sometimes bid for work that the auto companies had intended to subcontract (Katz 1992).

### *The Threat From Employment-At-Will*

As high-performance firms try to rewrite their effort bargains in response to global competition, they also face unanticipated, head-to-head competition from a new breed of domestic employment-at-will firms. Part of this shift to employment-at-will production is occurring through increased subcontracting, but much of it is coming from large and well-established firms that are switching from high-performance to employment-at-will practices.

The new employment-at-will firms do not pay the wage premiums of Fordist or high-commitment firms, preferring instead to keep wages as low as market competition will allow. Jobs with these firms are of indefinite duration and employment is quickly adjusted in response to changing demand. Management retains unrestricted prerogatives over work rules and the assignment of workers; no expectation of job security is offered; and no commitment from employees is expected.

Employment-at-will firms do relatively little human resources development and do not depend on effort bargains to motivate labor productivity. Instead, they rely on market incentives to motivate training investments and effort. Ironically, relying on market forces for a supply of skills has been made easier by the pool of surplus skilled and experienced labor released by downsizings and plant closings in the high-performance sector.

High-performance firms fear that their current attempts to develop more competitive effort bargains may fail, leaving them saddled with high wage and employment costs that are not being offset by productivity gains. In that event, they too are likely to switch to employment-at-will practices.

## The Turnaround in Unit Labor Costs

Broad-based measures of productivity and labor costs suggest that the competitive position of the American economy has been improving during this period of restructuring of the workplace training system. For example, productivity increases in manufacturing rebounded after 1980 as more aggressive productivity-improvement strategies came into play, almost doubling the annual increases of 1.8 percent a year during the period 1975–1980 when employment cost-cutting strategies were first introduced.

Unit labor costs, a summary indicator that includes the effects of both cost-cutting and productivity-improvement strategies, show a similar pattern. Between 1973 and 1979, unit labor costs climbed at an average annual rate of 6.1 percent before subsiding to an average of 1.1 percent a year during the decade of the 1980s. The decline in unit labor costs is especially remarkable in a number of mature industries. In nonelectrical machinery, unit labor costs in the 1980s fell at an annual rate of 5.2 percent, and there were also declines in women's apparel of 4.3 percent per year and in autos of two-tenths of a percent a year.

What cannot be determined, however, is the extent to which these improvements in cost competitiveness are the result of structural changes in high-performance workplaces that have enhanced labor productivity. The results could equally reflect cost-cutting reductions in effort bargains, the effects of closures of inefficient plants as markets declined, and a shift in the composition of production from high-wage, high-performance firms to lower-wage, employment-at-will firms.

## Can Public Policy Help?

While most of the changes affecting labor productivity have been the result of private actions taken by companies and unions, their consequences are a matter of deep public concern. For example, a recent study by the Commission on the Skills of the American Workforce (1990), a group that is reported to reflect the Clinton administration's thinking on workforce issues, concluded that raising productivity and restoring American living standards will depend on expanding high-performance employment. Three policy recommendations were identified as central to accomplishing this goal: (1) establishing a common threshold level of foundation skills for entry jobs; (2) creating a public system of skill training that would combine schooling with work experience; and (3) supporting increased workplace training and work reorganization through a 1 percent "play or pay" payroll tax.

In my view, however, such policies will not be sufficient to shift the balance in favor of high-performance firms. Raising foundation skills is a much overrated solution to the kinds of productivity problems facing high-performance firms. The foundations of productivity that are valued by such firms are not those of knowledge and skills, but involve workforce qualities such as flexibility, adaptability, teamwork, and problem-solving capacity. These are not the qualities that schools are used to training for, nor do they lend themselves to the setting of national standards for achievement.

Expanding public skill-training programs is also unlikely to foster an increase in the high-performance sector. Fordist and high-commitment firms have little difficulty recruiting the basic skills they need, and they often prefer to provide their own job training as part of effort bargains with their employees.

Where skill-training programs can make a difference, however, is in supplying trained labor to the employment-at-will sector. Employment-at-will firms want to hire workers who are job-ready, and they deliberately place the burden of human capital formation on workers and schools. As the employment-at-will sector expands, these training needs will grow.

Unfortunately, we lack the kinds of public sector skill-building institutions that can substitute for the lack of workplace training in the employment-at-will sector. With the exception of long-term residential programs such as the Jobs Corps, most government skill-training programs have yielded relatively little upgrading of skills, and the improvement in earnings has been correspondingly low (Taggart 1981; Bloom 1984; JTPA Advisory Committee 1989). Even the relatively well-financed programs for displaced workers have only been minimally effective (Podgursky and Swaim 1989; Seitchik and Zornitsky 1989).

A much talked-about new approach to skill training is the German model of apprenticeship training. The German "dual system," as it is called, blends technical and vocational schooling with on-the-job experience at a designated workplace. This system has been an effective source of skill training for young high school graduates in Germany, and there is a similar program for upgrading adult skills (Osterman 1991).

This German model, however, is unlikely to succeed in the United States, even if coupled with strong partnerships between schools and employers. An effective apprenticeship training program for the employment-at-will sector needs to be able to link training to the *highest common denominator* needs of *specific groups* of employers so that workers can easily transfer from one firm to another as employment shifts.

In contrast, school-based apprenticeships and other types of work and education partnerships in the United States have more typically gravitated towards the *lowest common denominator* training for entry jobs. Programs that have had more ambitious goals have usually been tailored to serve the needs of a single large employer. Rarely have these programs had any mechanism for ensuring *high-productivity* training for a *pool* of potential employers, and none have sought to facilitate labor mobility among such employers.

A more suitable model is apprenticeship programs that are jointly operated by unions and employer associations, such as those for craft workers in the building trades. Because craft unions represent the human capital interests of their members and have hiring commitments from a pool of employers, they can operate apprenticeship programs that meet the highest common denominator skill needs in their industry. Furthermore, because such programs involve groups of employers, they are well-suited to operate in the unstable and shifting markets of the employment-at-will sector. In principle, these programs could also meet the neglected training needs of small employers, who account for about one in five jobs in manufacturing.

The carrot and stick of a modest payroll tax, however, is unlikely to make much difference to the future of this type of apprenticeship programs. The track record of similar subsidies for workplace training suggests that such incentives are insufficient to leverage substantial changes in employment practices, let alone overcome employer resistance in the employment-at-will sector to participation in training programs that involve unions (Doeringer et al. 1991, ch. 1).

A more effective policy direction might be to encourage union organization in the employment-at-will sector. Training funds could then be used to subsidize both workplace training and school-based classroom training conducted under union-management apprenticeship programs. If desired, threshold competency standards for these programs could be set by the employers and workers who will be using the training. While such a proposal runs counter to much of the thrust of government policy towards unions over the past decade or so, it may be timely to rethink this entire policy area.

The idea that productivity growth can be achieved through partnerships among business, government, and labor is relevant to the high-performance sector as well, particularly in Fordist firms that rely on negotiations with unions to define productivity levels. Governments can contribute in important ways to the climate in which effort bargains are negotiated by encouraging the substitution of high-performance labor relations in place of adversarial collective bargaining.

An example of this approach is found in the experience of Jamestown, New York, where frequent strikes and outmoded union work rules were accelerating the decline of the city's industrial base. Through the mediation efforts of the city government, areawide labor-management committees were established to improve the labor-relations climate. These efforts in turn led to the creation of in-plant labor-management committees, which are reported to have successfully slowed the loss of manufacturing jobs during the 1970s by reducing strikes, improving productivity, and changing the image of the city as a "bad labor town" (Gittell 1992).

## Future Directions for Workplace Training and Productivity

The American workplace is at a critical juncture in terms of its contribution to labor productivity. Cost-cutting, restructuring, and productivity improvements are restoring competitiveness *in production* to many industries, but it is not clear what types of jobs and workplace training systems will survive.

Companies and unions across the country are now debating which workplace training system should guide productivity and wage determination into the next century. Will it be some version of the Fordist model that is evolving in autos and steel; will it be a high-commitment model with high wages, intensive human resources development, and some form of employment guarantee; will it involve a greater use of craft and apprenticeship training arrangements; or will it be the low-wage, low-productivity employment-at-will model?

Each of these systems implies a different type of commitment to human resources development and a different approach to generating productivity growth. Each places a distinct imprint on the adjustment process in terms of who is affected, how the costs of adjustment are divided between employers and workers, and the rate at which plant-level productivity will grow. Ultimately, these are choices between high- and low-productivity strategies at the workplace, which, in the aggregate, will translate into long-term choices between a high-growth path and a low-growth path for productivity and income in the national economy.

At present, high-performance models of all kinds are imperiled by continued downsizing, broken effort bargains, and competition from employment-at-will production. Despite widespread management and union interest in improving labor productivity and successful instances where workplace restructuring has raised labor efficiency (Katz, Kochan, and Gobeille 1983; Katz 1985; Cooke 1989), a recent survey of medium- and large-size companies found that only two in five were using high-performance workplace practices, and in only a quarter of these firms did high-performance practices apply to more than half of the workforce (Osterman 1993).

It therefore remains to be seen whether the high-performance workplace can survive long enough to gain a majority share in the U.S. labor market, or if the low-performance, employment-at-will model will prevail.

## References

American Society of Training Directors. 1989. *Workplace Basics: The Skills Employers Want.* Alexandria, VA: American Society of Training Directors.

Bell, L. 1989. "Explaining Union Concessions in the 1980s: Economic Factors or Structural Change?" Mimeo, Federal Reserve Bank of New York, October.

Berenbeim, R.E. 1986. *Company Programs To Ease the Impact of Shutdowns.* New York: The Conference Board.

Bloom, H. 1984. "Estimating the Effect of Job Training Programs Using Longitudinal Data: Ashenfelter's Findings Reconsidered," *Journal of Human Resources* 14, 4 (Fall): 544–56.

*Business Week.* 1988. "Human Capital," September 19.

Christensen, K. 1989. "Flexible Staffing and Scheduling in U.S. Corporations." Research Bulletin No. 240, The Conference Board, New York.

Cole, R.E. 1989. *Strategies For Learning.* Berkeley, CA: University of California Press.

Commission on the Skills of America's Workforce. 1990. *America's Choice: High Skills or High Wages.* Rochester, NY: National Center on Education and the Economy, June.

Commission on Workforce Quality and Labor Market Efficiency. 1989. *Investing in People.* Washington, DC: Government Printing Office.

Cooke, W.N. 1989. "Improving Productivity and Quality Through Collaboration," *Industrial Relations* 28 ( Spring): 299–319.

Denison, Edward F. 1985. *Trends In American Economic Growth.* Washington, DC: Brookings Institution.

Doeringer, Peter B., et al. 1991. *Turbulence in the American Workplace.* New York: Oxford University Press.

Gittell, R. 1992. *Renewing Cities.* Princeton, NJ: Princeton University Press.

Griliches, Zvi. 1988. "Productivity Puzzles and R&D, Another Nonexplanation," *Journal of Economic Perspectives* 2, 4 (Fall): 9–21.

Hecker, D.E. 1992. "Reconciling Conflicting Data on Jobs for College Graduates," *Monthly Labor Review* (July): 3–12.

Jorgenson, Dale W. 1988. "Productivity and Post-War U.S. Economic Growth," *Journal of Economic Perspectives* 2, 4 (Fall): 23–41.

JTPA Advisory Committee. 1989. *Working Capital.* Washington, DC: Government Printing Office.

Kaboolian, L. 1990. "Shifting Gears: Auto Workers Assess the Transformation of Their Industry." Ph.D. dissertation, University of Michigan, Ann Arbor.

Katz, H.C. 1985. *Shifting Gears: Changing Labor Relations in the U.S. Automobile Industry.* Cambridge, MA: MIT Press.

_____. 1992. "The Decentralization of Collective Bargaining: A Comparative Review and Analysis," Mimeo, New York State School of Labor and Industrial Relations, July 13.

Katz, Harry C., T. Kochan, and K.R. Gobeille. 1983. "Industrial Relations Performance, Economic Performance, and QWL Programs: An Interplant Analysis," *Industrial and Labor Relations Review* 37 (October): 3–17.

Katz, L.F., and L.H. Summers. 1989. "Industry Rents: Evidence and Implications," *Brookings Papers on Economic Activity, Microeconomics.*

Kochan, Thomas A., Harry C. Katz, and Robert B. McKersie. 1986. *The Transformation of American Industrial Relations.* New York: Basic Books.

Mishel, L., and J. Bernstein. 1993. *The State of Working America.* Armonk, NY: M.E. Sharpe.

Olson, M. 1988. "The Productivity Slowdown, the Oil Shocks, and the Real Cycle," *Journal of Economic Perspectives* 2, 4 (Fall): 43–69.

Osterman, P. 1991. "Is There A Problem With the Youth Labor Market and If So, How Should We Fix It?" Mimeo, Sloan School of Management, July.

_____. 1993. "The Diffusion of High Performance Work Organization: How Much and What Explains It?" Mimeo, Sloan School of Management, January.

Podgursky, Michael, and Paul Swaim. 1989. "Do More-Educated Workers Fare Better Following Job Displacement?" *Monthly Labor Review* (August): 43–46.

Ruhm, Christopher J. 1992. "Secular Changes in the Work and Retirement Patterns of Older Men." Working Paper No. ECO 921101, Center for Applied Research, University of North Carolina, November.

Seitchik, Adam, and Jeffrey Zornitsky. 1989. *From One Job to the Next: Worker Adjustment in a Changing Labor Market.* Kalamazoo, MI: W.E. Upjohn Institute for Employment Research.

Taggart, R.A. 1981. *A Fisherman's Guide: An Assessment of Training and Remediation Strategies.* Kalamazoo, MI: W.E. Upjohn Institute for Employment Research.

U.S. Congress, Joint Economic Committee. 1973. *Economic Growth and Total Capital Formation.* Washington, DC: Government Printing Office, February 18.

# Workplace Training in the United States

## Is It Underproduced?

Ann P. Bartel
*Columbia University*

Economists have long been interested in investigating the determinants and outcomes of investments in job training. Starting with the pathbreaking work by Jacob Mincer (1962), researchers have gone on to document how job training affects the careers of individuals through its impact on wage growth, turnover behavior, and unemployment experiences. Studies have also focused on the way in which job training improves the productivity of business organizations (Bartel, forthcoming; Holzer et al. 1993) as well as the competitiveness of nations (U.S. Congress 1990).

During the last few years, a perception has grown that American workers do not receive sufficient on-the-job training. Many have argued that government must take a more active role in the market for training. Indeed, much of the campaigning in the last presidential election focused on this issue. In this paper, I attempt to answer the question posed in the title. The plan of attack is as follows. I first review the data available from various sources on the amount of training that American workers receive and then analyze and compare workplace training in other countries to the American experience. The next section shows how data on rates of return to investments in job training can be used to determine if underinvestment exists, followed by analysis of the likely causes of underinvestment and evaluation of the various proposals that have been suggested as cures for the underinvestment problem. I then discuss my recent research on the relationship between technological change and training and show the implications of these research findings for the question posed in the title of this paper.

## What Do We Know About Workplace Training in the United States?

Our knowledge about the amount of workplace training in the United States is only as good as the quality of the available data on training. Two types of data sources can be consulted: surveys of individual workers and employer surveys. Training questions are included in the following surveys of individuals: the Current Population Survey, the Panel Study of Income Dynamics and the National Longitudinal Surveys of Mature Men, Young Men, Young Women, and Youth. The latter survey, the NLSY, is unique in the comprehensiveness of the training data reported. Data on a maximum of seven different training programs taken at any time since the last interview are included. Beginning with the 1988 survey, data on the following items are available for each of the seven training programs: when the respondent began and ended the training programs; what type of program it was, e.g., apprenticeships, company training, technical/vocational training off the job (such as business college, nurses programs, vocational and technical institutes, barber or beauty school, a correspondence course) and government training; and how many hours the respondent usually devoted per week to this program.[1] In the other surveys of individuals it is not possible to observe when the training actually took place or to measure the duration of the training.[2] Hence, the NLSY is the best employee-based source for measuring workplace training.

Table 1 provides some descriptive statistics from the NLSY. The table shows that in 1990, approximately 13 percent of the individuals in the sample received company training each year, and the duration of this training was 250 hours. The individuals in this sample are young, between the ages of 25 and 32 (in 1990), when most workplace training takes place. A comparable survey of older individuals would presumably find a much lower incidence of training. Table 1 also shows that education level is an important determinant of receipt of training. Only 7.4 percent of individuals with less than a high school education received company training, compared to 24.6 percent of college graduates. Individuals who work in large firms are more likely to receive company training compared to those in small firms; 21 percent of individuals employed by firms with at least 1,000 employees received

**Table 1. Incidence and Duration of Company Training by Education and Size of Firm, 1990 National Longitudinal Survey of Youth Aged 14–21 in 1979**

| | All education | | Education<12 | | Education=12 | | Education,13–15 | | Education 16+ | |
|---|---|---|---|---|---|---|---|---|---|---|
| | % trained | Mean hrs. if trained | % trained | Mean hrs. if trained | % trained | Mean hrs. if trained | % trained | Mean hrs. if trained | % trained | Mean hrs. if trained |
| All firms (N=4,311) | 13.4 | 251.13 | 7.4 | 198.15 | 10.3 | 269.53 | 18.0 | 225.13 | 24.6 | 257.00 |
| Large firms (N=1,470) | 20.9 | 259.12 | 11.1 | 177.32 | 15.3 | 279.33 | 24.4 | 211.35 | 35.6 | 300.51 |
| Small firms (N=2,841) | 9.5 | 225.78 | 6.2 | 209.96 | 7.7 | 259.94 | 13.7 | 241.77 | 16.2 | 183.92 |

NOTE: Large firms are defined as firms with at least 1,000 employees.

training compared to 9.5 percent of individuals in smaller firms. The picture painted by the data in table 1 is that company training is relatively uncommon; only 13 percent of individuals in the prime training years receive it, and it is concentrated among the highly educated working in large firms.

The second source of data, employer surveys, also paints a similar picture of small amounts of training. Lakewood Publications, the publishers of *Training Magazine*, reported that, based on a survey of 2,400 businesses, the aggregate expenditure on formal training was $45 billion in calendar year 1989. Averaged across the employed workforce, this implies an expenditure of $385 per worker. An alternative benchmark is that this expenditure equals 1.8 percent of total compensation in the United States.[3]

A major disadvantage of employer-based surveys is the low response rates on questions relating to the cost of employee training. Several years ago, Columbia Business School conducted a survey of human resource management practices in American businesses (Delaney, Ichniowski, and Lewin 1989). One part of the survey dealt with employee training and development, and businesses were asked whether they had a formal training program, and, if so, the annual cost per employee. Only 40 percent of the businesses that had formal training programs reported their annual cost. The probability of reporting the cost data was unrelated to the size of the business, return-on-assets, industry, capital/labor ratio, or the length of time the training program had been in operation (Bartel 1991). The problem seems to be that many businesses are not sure what costs should be included and/or they are unable to readily locate a cost measure for their organization. Aggregate cost data on employee training may, therefore, be an unreliable measure of the existence of underinvestment.

Workers in the United States receive training from sources other than formal company training programs, but the extent of participation is low. In the NLSY, 4.2 percent of the individuals reported receiving training in 1990 from one of the following sources: a business college, a vocational or technical institute, a barber or beauty school, or a correspondence course. Apprenticeships in this sample of individuals were relatively rare. In 1990, only 1 percent of the individuals in the NLSY reported receiving training through an apprenticeship program. This finding is not atypical of other data sources on apprenticeships in the

United States. For example, the U.S. Congress (1990) reports that, between 1970 and 1987, apprentices in federally registered programs fell from 0.3 percent of the United States civilian workforce to only 0.16 percent.

Informal on-the-job training, on the other hand, appears to be quite important for American workers. In the January 1991 Current Population Survey (U.S. Department of Labor 1992), 38 percent of the individuals who reported receiving skill improvement training on their current job indicated that the source of that training was informal on-the-job training. Formal company training was reported as the source of skill improvement training for another 38 percent of the individuals. The remaining 24 percent reported school or miscellaneous sources. Hence, according to this survey, participation in informal on-the-job training occurs with the same frequency as participation in formal company training programs.

When training is measured by hours rather than by incidence, there is some evidence that informal on-the-job training is more important than formal company training programs. A 1989 Columbia Business School survey of two hundred businesses found that, during their first three months on the job, employees in these businesses spent three times as many hours in informal training as they did in formal training (Bartel 1991). Using data from the 1982 Employment Opportunity Pilot Project, Barron, Black, and Loewenstein (1989) also found that, during the first three months of employment, time spent in informal training exceeded time spent in formal training.

## How Does the United States Compare to Other Countries?

One way of judging whether workplace training is adequately provided in the United States is to compare the experience of a typical American worker with that of a worker living in another country. In this section, I describe the provision of training in Germany, France, and Japan and show how training in these countries differs from the United States.

### *Germany*

At age 16 or the completion of grade 10, German students select a "career track." Approximately 60 percent of the students choose to end their schooling at this point and enter an apprenticeship program. The remaining 40 percent go on to universities or to careers in skilled white-collar occupations that require attendance at vocational colleges. There are 380 officially recognized occupations for which apprentice positions exist (Dowling and Albrecht 1991). Eighty percent of all German firms with at least twenty employees participate in apprenticeship programs (U.S. Congress 1990).

The apprenticeship contract signed by the company and the apprentice states that the company must train the worker in subject areas that are determined by the regulations governing a particular occupation. The federal government works with trade associations and unions to define uniform national curricula and examinations. The contract sets out the length of the initial trial period of the apprentice (during which either party can opt out of the contract) and his or her wages. The apprenticeship period usually lasts between two and three years and is split equally between practical training in the firm and vocational education at a vocational school run by the government. At the end of the apprenticeship period, the student must pass a final exam consisting of theoretical and practical parts, which then certifies the student to pursue the occupation. Ninety percent of the apprentices are employed by the firm that trained them.

In sum, apprenticeships are a formalized part of the German training system. If apprenticeships were to serve as an indicator of the extent of job training, we would conclude that the American worker is undertrained relative to the German worker. But, as we have already indicated, training is multidimensional, and it is impossible to conclude, based on available data, that German workers do indeed receive more training overall than American workers.[4]

### *France*

Unlike the German system of training which relies on apprenticeships, the French system has as its central component a mandated training tax. Since July 1971, employers with ten or more employees have been obligated to spend a certain percentage of their wage bill on continuing education and training of employees or pay a tax equal to the difference between the obligated and actual training expenditures. In 1971, this tax was 0.8 percent of the wage bill; as of January 1993, it is 1.4 percent. Unlike the situation in the United States, participation in formal company training is quite common in France. In 1990, 32 percent of all French employees received some formal company training (Bishop 1993). The incidence of training among young employees is likely to be higher than this number. Recall that in the United States, only 13 percent of individuals between the ages of 25 and 32 received formal company training in 1990. Although participation is much more extensive in France, formal training is of much shorter duration. In 1990, the average time spent in training by a trainee was only 46 hours! (The comparable figure for the United States is 250 hours.) There are some similarities between the American and French experiences. As in the United States, large French firms are more likely to provide formal training. In 1990, 53 percent of the employees in firms with at least 2,000 workers received training, compared to 8 percent of the employees in firms with 10–19 employees (Bishop 1993). There is also a positive relationship between skill level (education) and receipt of training. Whereas 50 percent of managers and professionals in French firms received formal company training in 1990, only 13 percent of unskilled operatives received it.

Hence, these data do not support the conclusion that French workers receive more training than American workers. While incidence of training is higher in France, duration is considerably smaller.

### *Japan*

The Japanese approach to training differs substantially from the German approach. In Japan, training is for a firm, not a trade. Large firms provide extensive workplace training, and there is minimal government involvement or assistance. The policy of providing continuous training for employees is largely grounded in the Japanese system of "lifetime employment" in large firms. A case study of American and Japanese autoworkers showed that autoworkers in Japanese plants receive three times as much training each year as workers in U.S. plants (U.S. Congress 1990).

While large firms in Japan provide extensive on-the-job training to their employees, only one-third of the Japanese labor force is employed by such firms. The remaining two-thirds work in small firms where lifetime employment is not guaranteed and training is not extensive.

## Rates of Return as Measures of Underinvestment in Training

As demonstrated above, a comparison of the U.S. training system with the systems used in other countries does not lead to an unambiguous conclusion that American workers are undertrained relative to their foreign counterparts. Here I approach the underinvestment question in a different way. In particular, I present data on the rates of return to job training for different groups of workers and consider whether the observed rates are too high. A rate of return above the rates on investments of comparable risk levels would enable us to conclude that underinvestment in job training does exist.

The rate of return that an employer earns on investment in employee training can be calculated by utilizing data on the costs of the training program and the returns that the employer receives. In order to calculate this accurately, the researcher would require information on the direct costs of the training program (i.e., instructors' salaries, materials, books, etc.), the time spent by trainees in the programs and the value of their lost productivity during the training period, and the increase in productivity that occurs after the training is completed and that can be attributed to participation in the training program. This is a very stringent list of requirements and can only be fulfilled if the researcher has access to a company that keeps good records and is willing to share the information.

I was fortunate to gain access to the personnel files and training database of a large manufacturing company. The direct costs of training were calculated from the company's records on the salaries of trainers, materials, and other expenses such as room and board for residential training programs. Indirect costs were calculated by multiplying the number of days spent in training by the daily salary earned by the employee prior to participation in the training program. The returns that the company earned from the training program were calculated from a fixed effects model which estimated the effect of time spent in the training program on salary (Bartel 1992).[5] If workers are assumed to stay "forever" in this company, the rate of return equals the ratio of the annual return to training divided by the sum of the direct and indirect costs of training. Table 2 shows that the calculated rate of return on training for this company is 21 percent. Of course, it is unrealistic to assume that workers stay forever at a company, and the rate of return needs to be adjusted to reflect the expected tenure at the company.[6] In this company, expected tenure is about ten years, and the adjusted rate of return equals 17 percent.

**Table 2. Rates of Return on Investments in Job Training**

| Sample | Assuming "lifetime employment" (percent) | Assuming "average" tenure[a] (percent) |
|---|---|---|
| National Longitudinal Survey of Youth | 32 | 16 |
| Panel Study of Income Dynamics[b] | 29 | 25 |
| Large manufacturing company[c] | 21 | 17 |

a. In this column, the rate of return is calculated by assuming that the payoff period for the investment equals the observed average length of tenure in the particular sample.
b. Mincer (1991).
c. Bartel (1992).

Admittedly these rates of return only pertain to one company and may not be generalizable to other companies in the United States. A more general estimate of the rate of return to job training in the United States can be calculated from national datasets on individuals. Unfortunately, with these datasets the cost of training may not be precisely measured. Information on direct costs of training are, of necessity, unavailable in datasets on individuals. The indirect costs of training can be inferred from data on the average amount of time spent in training by individuals who reported receiving training during the last year. Table 2 shows that in the NLSY sample, the calculated rate of return is

32 percent if the individuals are assumed to stay with their employers "forever," but that the rate of return falls to 16 percent when it is adjusted for expected tenure. Since the individuals in this sample are young, their expected tenure is only three years; this produces a large drop in the adjusted rate of return. Mincer (1991) calculated the rates of return on training for the individuals in the Panel Study of Income Dynamics, and I report those rates as well in table 2. The unadjusted rate is 29 percent and the adjusted rate is 25 percent.

The adjusted rates in table 2 range from 16 percent to 25 percent. These rates seem high when compared to other investments. For example, Bound and Johnson (1992) calculate that the private rate of return on a year of schooling is currently about 8.5 percent in the United States.[7] Using this number as a benchmark would lead to a conclusion that there is underinvestment in job training. It is possible, however, that the estimated rates of return on training may be overestimates of the true rates. This could occur if the true cost of training is underestimated or the returns on training are overestimated because of incomplete controls for unobserved heterogeneity or overly optimistic estimates of a worker's expected tenure.

## What Can Account for Underinvestment in Training?

If we use the rates of return reported in the previous section as evidence that workplace training in the United States is underproduced, we next need to consider why this underinvestment takes place. Armed with this analysis, we can then proceed to make informed policy recommendations to increase investment in training.

It has been argued (Bishop 1991) that American workers receive less training than their German and Japanese counterparts because the turnover rate is higher in the United States. The OECD (1984) reports that, for employees with less than one year of tenure, the probability of staying at the firm for at least twelve additional months is over 80 percent in the United Kingdom, 76 percent in Japan but only 41 percent in the United States. In Germany, 95 percent of apprentices who complete the three-month probationary period stay with their employer for the full three-year apprenticeship period (Bishop 1991). The typical pattern of a young American worker is to engage in job shopping during the early years in the labor market. High rates of turnover will reduce the firm's incentive to invest in specific training. Bishop (1991) shows that employers also pay part of the costs of general training, and the expectation of high turnover will therefore also reduce the firm's incentive to provide general training.

Another factor contributing to less training in the United States is the difficulty that American employers have in assessing the quality of an applicant's general skills. In Germany, standardized curricula and national certification standards provide employers with reliable information on a job applicant's skills. In the United States, employers do not give enough weight to an applicant's stock of general skills. The result is that American workers have less incentive to invest in general skills.

The constraint imposed by the minimum wage reduces the incentive for firms to invest in training workers whose value of marginal product is less than the legislated minimum wage. This happens because the workers are unable to offer to pay for general training by accepting a wage below the minimum wage. Leighton and Mincer (1981) provide evidence that the minimum wage leads to less on-the-job training for low-skilled young workers than would otherwise occur. While it is true that employers are now able to pay a subminimum training wage to employees under the age of 20 for the first six months of their employment, this does not address the problem faced by unskilled workers aged 20 and over.[8]

A fourth reason for underinvestment is that young workers are unable to pay for the general skills that they need because they are liquidity-constrained. Since firms have no incentive to pay for general training (except, perhaps, because of the positive effect on their reputations), young workers must subsidize their own training and often have insufficient funds to do so.

Finally, it has been argued (U.S. Congress 1990) that American workers may receive less training than German and Japanese workers because they have poor basic skills. According to the Office of Technology Assessment, American companies find that, in their operations in Germany or Japan, workers have better reading and math skills than Americans in the United States. The absence of good basic skills makes the American worker less trainable, thereby reducing the perceived return on the company's investment in training.

## Policy Options to Increase Investment in Training

In this section I review and evaluate a number of policy recommendations that have been suggested to increase employee and employer investments in on-the-job training. The first idea is that training should be provided by the government. The obvious criticism of this proposal is that the government will not have adequate information to know what types of skills businesses need in their employees.

A second approach is to adopt the French system whereby a payroll-based national training tax is imposed on all employers. Under this system, employers would either spend the mandated percentage amount on training or pay a tax equal to the difference between the obligated and actual training expenditures. While this approach is preferable to direct provision of training by the government because it allows the firm to decide on the amount and type of training, it suffers from a number of problems. First, there is no incentive for firms to spend beyond the mandated level. Second, it favors large firms because of economies of scale in the provision of formal training. Third, it completely ignores informal training, and we have already seen that informal training is a significant component of total training. Firms that find it optimal to rely on informal training would be penalized under this system. Fourth, there would be significant measurement problems as firms and the government debate what types of activities qualify as training.

A third approach is for the federal government to provide subsidies to firms that engage in training. This is more appealing than the mandate approach because it does not require firms to spend a stipulated amount; firms would enjoy more flexibility in making the optimal choice. The federal government's Job Training Partnership Act created a system to share the costs of training new employees with private firms. Unfortunately, recent reports (*Business Week* 1992) have documented misuse of JTPA funds. In particular, firms have been accused of using JTPA funds to cover the costs of "training" workers who were already trained, as well as unreasonably extending the length of a worker's training period.

A number of states have training subsidy programs, and the evidence regarding the impact of these programs is, unlike the JTPA, generally positive. Creticos and Sheets (1990) studied the programs that exist in New York, Illinois, California, and Missouri and found that in twenty-four companies that received financial aid from the states, all of the companies showed improvements in business performance from the training. Holzer et al. (1993) have studied the training grant program operated in Michigan during 1988 and 1989, called the Michigan Job Opportunity Bank-Upgrade Program. They found that firms that received training grants significantly increased the amount of training they provided their employees; in other words, the subsidies did not simply provide windfalls to those firms already engaging in training. But the experiences with JTPA indicate that a government subsidy program will require careful monitoring to avoid abuse.

Another idea that has been suggested is that the government should subsidize the creation of employer training collectives (U.S. Congress 1990). The purpose of these collectives would be for firms in an industry to jointly provide the skills necessary for that industry. By sharing the costs and risks of providing training, firms would have an incentive to train more. The disadvantage of this approach is that firms in an industry may be concerned about sharing proprietary information. Also, free-riders outside the consortia could attempt to raid the newly trained workers.

Finally, there are some government programs that can be introduced to increase the incentive for the employee to invest in general training. Like the German government, the U.S. government can work with industry and trade groups to establish national certification standards for various trades and occupations. This will enable employers to assess the quality of the general skills an applicant possesses. In addition, the federal government could consider providing low-cost loans to individuals who wish to acquire general skills. Alternatively, a revision of the current tax law that pertains to the deductibility of an employee's own training expenses could be considered. At the present time, if an employee pays for his or her own training, the expenses can only be deducted if the sum of those expenses plus all other miscellaneous deductions exceeds 2 percent of an individual's adjusted gross income.

## The Role of Technological Change

The programs discussed in the previous section are attempts to address perceived flaws in the U.S. market for training. Each of the suggested programs strives to increase training by either circumventing the market entirely, subsidizing the costs incurred by trainees or trainers, or improving the quality of information in the labor market.

It is possible, however, that the future for the U.S. training market is brighter than we currently think. The ratio of expenditures on company-sponsored R&D to net sales has been increasing in the United States in recent years (National Science Foundation 1989). Rates of productivity growth in the 1980s are far ahead of the rates observed in the late 1970s (U.S. Department of Labor 1992). All of this bodes well for the training of American workers because, in a world in which firms are updating or changing their production technologies, the opportunities for learning expand. When firms are introducing new technologies, they have an incentive to train their employees in order to reap the productivity gains from the technological change. A formal way of stating this argument is that the marginal cost of producing a unit of human capital investment decreases with technological change (Tan 1989).

Some people may take a more pessimistic view of the relationship between technological change and training. The basis for the pessimistic view is that technological change increases the rate at which human capital depreciates. Within the Ben-Porath (1967) framework, higher rates of depreciation reduce the marginal return to investment and thereby lead to less investment in on-the-job training in each time period. The theoretical prediction about the impact of technological change on the amount of on-the-job training is ambiguous.

In my paper with Nachum Sicherman (Bartel and Sicherman 1993), I conducted an empirical analysis that resolves the theoretical ambiguity. We used the 1979–1990 National Longitudinal Surveys of Labor Market Experience of Youth aged 14–21 in 1979 to analyze whether individuals who work in industries that are technologically progressive receive more training, *ceteris paribus*. Since our study covers both the manufacturing and nonmanufacturing sectors, we measure an industry's rate of technological change by its rate of productivity change as calculated by Jorgenson, Gollop, and Fraumeni (1987). Ideally, one would prefer to use R&D intensity as the measure of technological change in the industry, but R&D data are only available for the manufacturing sector. Griliches and Lichtenberg (1984) have shown that for the time period 1959–1976 there was a significant relationship between an industry's intensity of private R&D expenditures and subsequent growth in productivity. Lichtenberg and Siegel (1991) also found that this relationship existed at the company level in the 1970s and 1980s.

In our study, we estimated an equation in which the dependent variable is the probability of receiving company training since the last survey (i.e., during the last year) and the independent variables are (1) the mean rate of technological change in the individual's industry during the ten years prior to the date of the interview, and (2) a vector of control variables that includes education, experience and its square, tenure and its square, size of plant in which the individual works, marital status, race, union membership, and residence in an SMSA. We found that, in industries with higher rates of technological change, employees are significantly more likely to receive company training.

If rates of technological change continue to increase over the next decade as they have during the last five years, these findings would predict an increase in the amount of training that U.S. workers will receive. This will not require tampering with the U.S. training market by imposing targets for training, nor will it require an expenditure of government funds to subsidize the cost of training. Rather, an increase in employee training will be a simple by-product of increased rates of technological change and expenditures on R&D.

## Summary and Conclusions

I began this paper by posing the question of whether or not workplace training in the United States is underproduced. In order to answer this question, it was necessary to carefully review the data available on the extent of workplace training in the United States. Since company data are generally sparse, researchers must rely on surveys of individuals that include questions on workplace training. These data show that only 13 percent of individuals in the prime training years (ages 25–32) received formal company training in the United States in 1990, and that this training was concentrated among the highly educated working in large firms. Apprenticeships are rare in the United States. Informal on-the-job training appears to be at least as important as formal company training.

The training experience of the American worker is very different from that of workers in other countries. But, specific comparisons with Germany, France, and Japan do not enable us to unambiguously conclude that American workers, in general, receive less training than their counterparts in those countries. An alternative approach to the underinvestment question is to consider whether the observed rates of return on investments in job training are too high. We found that rates are indeed high when compared to rates of return to education in the United States. Underinvestment in job training could be due to high turnover, the absence of standardized curricula and national certification standards for occupations, minimum wage constraints, liquidity constraints, and/or weak basic skills of American workers. Each of these causes suggests a proposed solution, and we reviewed and critiqued a number of these: (1) direct provision of training by the government, (2) a payroll-based national training tax similar to the system used in France, (3) government subsidies to firms that train their workers, (4) employer training collectives, and (5) low-cost loans and tax breaks for individuals who pay for their own training.

While the high rates of return to training may be consistent with a yes answer to the question posed in the title, I ended with an optimistic forecast for the future of the training market. Research evidence has shown that technological change increases the incentives for investment in training. If the recent upward trends in R&D expenditures and productivity growth rates in the U.S. continue, we can predict that opportunities for training will increase. The attractiveness of this scenario is that the increase in training will not require government interference with the training market.

# NOTES

1. Prior to 1988, detailed information on type of private sector training, as well as the weeks and hours per week spent in training, were only recorded if the training spell lasted at least four weeks.

2. In the National Longitudinal Surveys of Young and Older Men and Young Women, the survey asks, "What was the longest type of training you have had since the last interview?" In the Current Population Survey, the question is, "What training was needed to get the current or last job and what training is needed to improve skills on the current job?"

3. In France, expenditures on formal company training equal 3 percent of total compensation.

4. In the report prepared by the U.S. Congress (1990), evidence is presented that workers in German metalworking firms receive more training than comparable workers in British metalworking firms. No evidence is presented, however, that beyond the apprenticeship period, German workers receive more training than American workers.

5. The profitability of training is actually the increase in productivity less the increase in wages. Barron, Black, and Loewenstein (1989) and Blakemore and Hoffman (1988) show that productivity doubles compared to wages in the datasets that they analyze. This implies that the wage increase attributable to training is a good proxy for the productivity increase produced by training.

6. Mincer (1991) shows that adjusted rate of return is calculated by the following formula: $r = r^1(1 - (1/1{+}r)^T)$ where $T$ = expected tenure and $r$ is the adjusted rate of return.

7. This does not include the consumption returns to schooling. If these were added in, the rate of return on schooling would increase, and may approach the rate of return on training.

8. In an analysis of the fast food industry, Katz and Krueger (1992) provide evidence that the subminimum training wage is rarely used.

## References

Barron, John M., Dan A. Black, and Mark A. Loewenstein. 1989. "Job Matching and On-the-Job Training," *Journal of Labor Economics* 7 (January): 1–19.

Bartel, Ann P. 1991. "Employee Training Programs in U.S. Businesses." In *Market Failure in Training? New Economic Analysis and Evidence on Training of Adult Employees,* David Stern and Jozef Ritzen, eds. New York: Springer-Verlag.

_____. 1992. "Training, Wage Growth and Job Performance: Evidence from a Company Database." NBER Working Paper No. 4027, March.

_____. Forthcoming. "Productivity Gains from the Implementation of Employee Training Programs," *Industrial Relations.*

Bartel, Ann P., and Nachum Sicherman. 1993. "The Impact of Technological Change on Training and Job Mobility of Young Workers." Mimeo. Columbia University Graduate School of Business, February.

Ben-Porath, Yoram. 1967. "The Production of Human Capital and the Life Cycle of Earnings," *Journal of Political Economy* 75 (August): 352–365.

Bishop, John. 1991. "Underinvestment in On-the-Job Training?" Working Paper No. 91–03, Cornell University Center for Advanced Human Resource Studies, January.

———. 1993. "Underinvestment in Employer Training: Is a Mandate the Answer?" Working Paper No. 93–02, Cornell University Center for Advanced Human Resource Studies, January.

Blakemore, Arthur, and Dennis Hoffman. 1988. "Seniority Rules and Productivity: An Empirical Test." Mimeo. Arizona State University.

Bound, John, and George Johnson. 1992. "Changes in the Structure of Wages During the 1980s: An Evaluation of Alternative Explanations." *American Economic Review* 82, 3: 371–382.

*Business Week.* 1992. "90 Days to Learn to Scrub? Sure, If Uncle Sam's Paying," January 20.

Creticos, Peter A., and Robert G. Sheets. 1990. "Evaluating State-Financed, Workplace-Based Retraining Programs." National Commission for Employment Policy and the National Governors' Association.

Delaney, John, Casey Ichniowski, and David Lewin. 1989. "Human Resource Management Policies and Practices in American Firms." Report submitted to the Bureau of Labor-Management Relations and Cooperative Programs, U.S. Department of Labor.

Dowling, Michael J., and Karl-Otto Albrecht. 1991. "Technical Workers and Competitive Advantage: What We Can Learn from the Germans," *Business Horizons* (November/December).

Griliches, Zvi, and Frank Lichtenberg. 1984. "R&D and Productivity Growth at the Industry Level: Is There Still a Relationship?" In *R&D, Patents, and Productivity,* Zvi Griliches, ed. Cambridge: NBER.

Holzer, Harry J., Richard N. Block, Marcus Cheatham, and Jack H. Knott. 1993. "Are Training Subsidies for Firms Effective? The Michigan Experience," *Industrial and Labor Relations Review* 46, 4: 625–36.

Jorgenson, Dale W., Frank M. Gollop, and Barbara M. Fraumeni. 1987. *Productivity and U.S. Economic Growth.* Cambridge: Harvard University Press.

Katz, Lawrence, and Alan Krueger. 1992. "The Effect of the Minimum Wage on the Fast Food Industry." NBER Working Paper No. 3997, February.

Leighton, Linda, and Jacob Mincer. 1981. "The Effects of Minimum Wages on Human Capital Formation." In *The Economics of Legal Wages,* Simon Rottenberg, ed. Washington, DC: American Enterprise Institute.

Lichtenberg, Frank, and Donald Siegel. 1991. "The Impact of R&D Investment on Productivity: New Evidence Using Linked R&D-LRD Data," *Economic Inquiry* 29 (April): 203–228.

Lynch, Lisa. 1992. "Private-Sector Training and the Earnings of Young Workers," *American Economic Review* 82 (March): 299–312.

Mincer, Jacob. 1962. "On-the-Job Training: Costs, Returns and Some Implications," *Journal of Political Economy,* Supplement 70 (October): 50–79.

_____. 1991. "Job Training: Costs, Returns and Wage Profiles." In *Market Failure in Training? New Economic Analysis and Evidence on Training of Adult Employees,* David Stern and Jozef Ritzen eds. New York: Springer-Verlag.

National Science Foundation. 1989. "National Patterns of R&D Resources: 1989." Final Report, NSF 89–308.

Organization of Economic Cooperation and Development (OECD). 1984. *Employment Outlook,* Paris: OECD, September, Chapter 4.

Tan, Hong W. 1989. "Technical Change and Its Consequences for Training and Earnings." Manuscript, RAND Corporation.

U.S. Congress. 1990. *Worker Training: Competing in the New International Economy,* Office of Technology Assessment, OTA-ITE-457. Washington, DC: Government Printing Office, September.

U.S. Department of Labor. 1992. "How Workers Get Their Training: A 1991 Update." BLS Bulletin 2407, August.

_____. 1993. "Productivity and Costs." USDOL 93–79, March 9.

# The Very-Long-Run Effect of Human Capital on Human Progress

Julian L. Simon
*University of Maryland*

This article is my first attempt to state a general theory of human progress in connection with the concept of population numbers and human capital. The theory is presented with only a sketchy formal framework and with little supporting data; those elements must await a longer presentation.

The question addressed here is: What is the rock bottom cause of so many of the world's population now being long-lived and endowed with much wealth and a high standard of living, with an even larger proportion likely to enjoy these benefits in the coming decades, whereas people did not have those advantages 10,000, 2,000, 1,000, or even 200 years ago? The obvious answer—almost a definition—is that current technology $A_{1993}$ is a sum of increments to knowledge $dA$ in the past. And these $dA$ were produced by people and therefore must have been influenced by human numbers. One may add that the cultural, political, economic, and social systems of the past were also a factor, and perhaps a more important factor than numbers. I shall argue, however, that those systems were themselves a function of human numbers together with the economic levels of past societies; this is one of the main points of the paper.

Why did the rapid progress of the past two centuries not begin centuries or millennia earlier, or not begin until sometime in the future? Was there something extraordinary about the human numbers $P$ or the level of technology $A$ in the year 1700 or so? Probably not. But we must notice one crucial correlation: Both $P$ and $A$ as well as the income $Y$ all began to rise rapidly about that time. That rise represented an unprecedented tripling or more within a century or two and was the first such event in all the thousands of years of human history.

The answer I offer is that the size of the human population, as measured by both population density *P*/ln*d* and *P* together with the technology these people produced, is the root cause of the speed of progress. More operationally, if the world's population had not grown at all since, say, 10,000 years ago, or if population had not grown as fast as it did over the millennia, the material condition of humanity could not have progressed to its present state. To put it differently, if the rate of population growth had been different (and had resulted in different total populations at various times) than actually was the case, the extraordinary period of the past two hundred years of falling mortality and increasing income would have happened either much later or much earlier. Furthermore, one cannot say this of any other variable unless it would primarily alter human numbers—as, for example, a climatic change would have affected food production, or the quantity of energy easily available would have improved survival probabilities. If there were not an effect on human numbers, such a change would have affected the amount of leisure and perhaps the mode of getting a living, for example, herding versus hunting, but would not have affected the speed of economic progress.

Even bestowing a library of today's knowledge upon a small population in the past probably would not have led to rapid progress. Indeed, we know from the experience of India and China and other poor countries until recently that the existence of such knowledge can coexist with continuing backwardness. This leads to the question of whether that fact does not contradict the basic thesis of this paper. I think it does not, because we already see the inexorable process of rapid modernization in these countries, despite having economic-political-social systems not well designed for such progress, systems that kept the modernization from happening earlier (as it happened earlier in Japan). And in turn, the combination of numbers and the existence of knowledge, together with the demand for the fruits that knowledge brings about, are inducing huge changes in the economic systems so as to accommodate more rapid progress, as the thesis in this paper suggests; this has been the case most vividly for 700 million rural Chinese whose agriculture was essentially privatized starting in 1979. So, taken altogether the evidence available as of 1993 concerning the poor though well-populated countries is not inconsistent with the thesis offered here.

Two lines of evidence are adduced to support the basic proposition: (1) correlations of population size *P* and density *P*/ln*d* with the rate of knowledge production *dA*, and (2) evidence that other relevant variables are a function of *P* and *Y*. I also present some scrappy evidence to show that population is not only correlated with knowledge production but also is a causal variable. And I present theory and data to disprove the proposition that the "natural" availability of natural resources has been a crucial force.

I will argue (in connection with the causal concept used here) that there is no nonbiological variable "deeper" than human numbers that one can point to as being responsible for the population growth that occurred, as one can point to population growth as being responsible for the growth in income and the evolution of institutions and patterns of behavior that were necessary for the progress that occurred. That is, I will argue that unlike all other nonbiological variables, population growth is exogenous in the process.

Many laypersons would say (and I agree with them) that the proposition stated here is entirely obvious: If there were no people, there would be no "human capital" to create the knowledge that leads to progress, and hence there would be no progress. But this answer is not at all obvious or agreed-to in the view of many scholars, when speaking of long-run as well as of short-run progress. So the work required here is not the demolition of a strawman.

It is a crucial element of the model stated here that population growth and density affect the structure of law and tradition and political institutions. If this were not so, structures that are incompatible with an improvement in technology and the long-run standard of living could have remained in place indefinitely, thereby preventing further progress. It is therefore an important part of this essay—and perhaps its most important novelty—to offer fine-structure evidence for this process of population-induced social change.

The complex web of relationships of endemic and epidemic disease, and knowledge of them, with population density and total numbers also is an important part of the analysis.

The strategy of the article will be as follows. The next section presents the theory offered here. I then review the skimpy time-series and cross-sectional evidence on the relationship of population to the rate of economic growth in the long run, and ask about the possibility that other variables could explain the observed long-run economic growth; at best, these data make a *prima facie* but not a compelling case for the theory. Next I digress to explore one particular topic which has been at the root of thinking about population economics for three thousand years: the relationship of numbers of people to supplies of natural resources. I follow that with a presentation of evidence on the relationship of population to structural factors that affect the rate of economic progress; this section is the heart of the paper; if given the space that the subject deserves, the section would take up most of the book which this subject properly requires (and which may yet come forth if luck holds).

Various sections draw heavily upon my earlier work on the subject of population growth; this article may be thought of as part of an evolutionary process in knowledge development.

## A Stylized Description of Human Progress

In order to set the scene before launching into more formal work, here is a stylized description of the long-run history of the process of human progress. The first hominids came into being without any body of knowledge that they themselves created, but instinctive knowledge of how to survive was programmed into their genes just as with every other species. And the early people may have learned some additional techniques by observing other animals that happened to live within their ken, such as techniques of building shelters and gathering food. Such imitations may have been the first sort of learning that is distinctively human in its cumulative adaptation to the world about us. (I have recently read that there seems to be a similar process of imitation among apes, but it is questionable whether the knowledge can be handed down from one generation to the next.)

The hominids then increased their population, just as other new species (if successful) increase their populations by spreading across new territory into niches that will sustain them. At some point—whether population had stabilized by that time or not is unknown—new discoveries were made. These discoveries might have included the knowledge of fire and of stone implements—the latter occurring at least two million years ago, according to Leakey (1981, p. 78). Each discovery improved the ability of our ancestors to survive and allowed numbers to increase faster than before the discovery; even simple stone tools must have had a large effect on the rate of population growth. (Fire and stone tools are "invention-pull" rather than "population-push" technology, requiring no increase in labor and therefore being of immediate utility rather than waiting for further population growth to make them profitable.) But recent work with genetics suggests that about 65,000 years ago the population was only about 100,000 and declined to about 10,000 before expanding again ("Research News," *Science*, October 1, 1993).

Why did rapid economic progress not occur much earlier—say 100,000 or a million years ago? Was it just an accident that rapid progress ever began, and could that accident just as easily have taken place many millennia earlier? I think not; I cannot imagine any single event that could have come along and made a big difference at an earlier time. The early invention of nuclear power obviously is inconceivable, but even had a nuclear reactor and full instructions been dropped on earth by Martians, it would have been less use than a meteorite. Utilization of nuclear power had to wait for the accumulation of the nexus of human numbers and knowledge.

Only a biological or environmental difference that would have altered the nutrition and/or the rate of fertility and of subsequent survival—either climate or the appearance of a remarkable new easy-to-obtain food source (or the opposite) or a change in the digestive system, for example—could have altered the speed of economic progress through the millennia. If numbers had been greater earlier on, there would have been more people to invent and develop new discoveries such as new ways of herding and cropping. Larger numbers also would have meant greater need for such improvements earlier on, which would have speeded up their adoption after invention in those cases where adoption is not immediately profitable (Boserupian population-push inventions).

Other kinds of differences could not have changed the rate of progress, I contend. The earliest hominids had elements of a social system in their genetic programs, just as do apes; for example, incest was surely practiced only infrequently, as with other species of animals. But while there must have been some variations in social system from one band of hominids to another, it would not have been possible for them to live with a modern form of social system that is consistent with modern rates of rapid progress, such as democracy, over an area as large as hundreds or even tens of miles in each direction, even if someone had invented it; such modern systems could not be used until population and technology (and the standard of living) had increased many times over.

Would history have been very different if numbers had stayed at the level they were at the time of Athens' glory? I contend that we would not have reached the technology and the standard of living we now enjoy—especially our unprecedented life expectancy, which began to lengthen rapidly only 250 years ago—if our numbers had remained at the few hundreds of millions on earth at the peak of Rome and Greece.

This essay is an attempt to support with theory and data the thoughts sketched out in the above paragraphs.

## The Theoretical Framework

My thesis is that (1) higher density and (2) larger total populations, in individual societies and on earth altogether, were *necessary* conditions for progress. The extent to which they were (and are) also *sufficient* conditions depended in the past upon the nature of the societies at the time. Particular societies certainly have been capable of *retrogression* in the face of population growth. The analysis suggests, though it cannot constitute more than a speculation on the matter, that conditions of twentieth century transportation and communications have rendered such long-term retrogression less and less likely, however.

The appropriate form for the inquiry is to ask: What would be the effect of a major change in some variable *x*? For example, what effect would there have been if the Anglo-Saxon legal system had somehow been transmitted to North American natives in the year 1000? Would this have had a major effect on their economic and demographic growth? The theory points to variables that are the key conditions of readiness for growth—the nexus of population numbers together with the stock of knowledge and the level of the standard of living.

An alternative theory, which I believe to be less compelling than the theory stated above, is that the invention of new knowledge *by itself* would raise the standard of living. For example, if starting in, say, the year 1000 societies had somehow decided to educate a much larger number of people and then put them to work in knowledge-producing pursuits, would that have raised the rate of progress of the living standard? Surely there would have been some increase in progress, but how much? The work of Boserup (1965), together with my analysis of inventions into those that are and are not immediately adopted without appropriate demand conditions (Simon 1977, chapter 8; 1978; and 1992, chapter 3), shows that some newly invented knowledge can remain dormant for a long time if demographic conditions are not appropriate for its adoption at the time.

A secondary and related thesis is that the income level of a society is the other most important determinant of significant material and technical variables such as health, knowledge, physical and social mobility, and communications. I will not develop this thesis here.

### *Conceptual Frameworks and the Time Horizon*

The appropriate conceptual framework for the analysis of the effects of population depends upon the length of horizon and upon the level of economic development (which has the aggregate in the long-run correlate with the historical date). These are some of the relevant frameworks.

1. For the very short run in a *subsistence* society, the framework of Malthus is appropriate; the coming of more mouths or a deterioration of natural conditions leads to diminishing returns in agriculture and causes there to be less to eat for the average person. For the very short run in a *developed* economy, the appropriate framework is a system of equations which may have hundreds of variables and thousands of connections, as seen in the spaghetti-like large-scale multisector models used for forecasting by consultants to government and business. In these short-run models for both subsistence and developed economies, the stock of technology and the nature of institutions—and sometimes even the size of the labor force—are considered fixed.

2. Somewhat longer-term models consider physical and human capital to vary. The growth of technology usually is considered to occur at

a constant rate. The structures of political institutions, law, work behavior, and tradition are considered to be fixed. The income level and the size of the labor force are important variables in such models.

3. An even longer-run model of a subsistence society allows for the nonconstant endogenous introduction of new technology. The alternative frameworks of the long-run Malthusian dynamics (quite different from the short-run Malthusian model mentioned above) and of the Boserup analysis for subsistence agriculture are complementary rather than opposing, as we shall see below. For developed economies, the recent crop of endogenous-growth models (including my own work on endogenous knowledge in connection with population growth) make technology endogenous, but do not include some of the variables included in the shorter-run models. These endogenous-growth models include only income, population, and knowledge as independent variables, and consider the structures of law and tradition only peripherally, if at all. Population growth may or may not be endogenous in this sort of model.

4. The longest-run model, the heart of this paper, contains population growth at the earliest date in the dynamic system as the sole exogenous variable; the structures of law, tradition, and other institutions are endogenous variables, along with the standard of living, technology, and subsequent population growth. From such a model one can deduce the proposition that if biological or climatological elements had caused the rate of population growth to be faster than it actually was, humanity would have had greater numbers than actually existed at various times in the past; and each state in its development, including the present state of high material culture and low mortality, would therefore have reached centuries or millennia earlier.

### *Population and Knowledge*

The most difficult analytic issue concerns the relationship between the causal roles of population and of knowledge. They are the only two variables about which one can reasonably say: If the stock of this variable had been much lower than its actual stock in year $t$, the state of humanity would have been vastly poorer in the year $t + x$ than it actually was. All other variables, such as the stocks of private physical capital and prime farmland, are likely to be replaced rather quickly if there is a sudden catastrophic loss; not so with population and knowledge.

The rock bottom causal element of long-run human progress is the combination of population and knowledge. They are as much inseparable parts of the same process as are the brain and the sexual organs. It makes as little sense to ask which is the "original" cause as about chicken and egg. Even the earliest humankind could not have survived and grown without such technology as cutting tools and fire; and in turn, the knowledge of these techniques came from human beings.

Indeed, the interpenetration of population and technology is shown by the fact that history consists of both the Boserupian "population-push" and the Malthusian "invention-pull" combinations of an invention and population growth, in which causation runs from one of these two forces in one case and to it in the other. (In Simon 1977, chapter 8; 1978; and 1992, chapter 3, I provide geometric and arithmetic theory for these two processes, together with extensive historical examples.)

The key point is that no *other* element was as essential as the combination of knowledge and human numbers—not institutions, law, physical capital, natural resources, or any other element. Humankind could live in a variety of settings of these variables and produce livable forms of them when they are completely absent; not so with knowledge and human numbers.

## Evidence on the Long-Run Progress-Population Connection

This section reviews the available time-series and cross-sectional evidence on the relationship of population to the rate of economic growth in the long run. The purpose is to show that there is indeed a connection to be investigated; these data make a *prima facie* case for the theory, but it is only *prima facie* and not a compelling case; to make a persuasive case requires the later sections of the paper. Then there is discussion of the possibility that variables other than population could explain the observed long-run economic growth.

## *Population Size and the Standard of Living*

*Time-series evidence.*

The first set of time-series evidence is stylized figures of crucial variables over the very long run. The purpose of the graphs is to show how all these variables moved in much the same general way, with population moving earlier than the others. The lack of any precise data and the consequent absence of ups and downs in the series prevents any explicit statistical exploration of causality.

For the longest period of the existence of human beings as a species—from, say, 20,000 years ago until 6,000 or 7,000 years ago—population growth was very slow, and hence total population and population density were low. This growth might be described by a straight line if plotted on semilog paper, but such a plot would obscure the point of the graph, which is that the rate of early growth was infinitesimal.

A slightly less broad view is shown in figure 1, whose logarithmic scale reveals the rapid increases in population starting with the onset of the agricultural, industrial, and postindustrial "revolutions."

**Figure 1. Growth of the Human Population of the World Over the Last One Million Years**

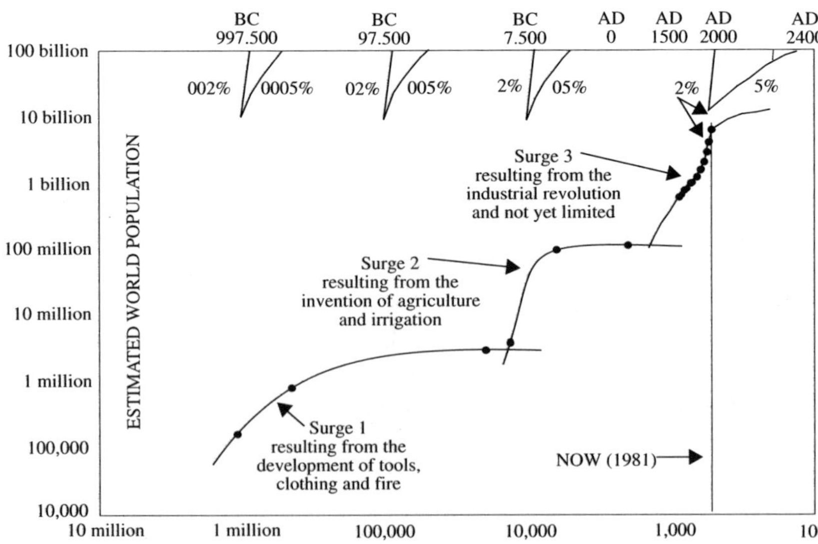


SOURCE: After Deevey 1960, by Tinsley 1980, p. 11.
NOTE: Please notice that the axes are logarithmic.

During most of the past millennia, economic progress undoubtedly was slow or nonexistent (which is proven by jobbing backwards; spreading total growth over such a long period of time implies a very low average rate), though it is very difficult to find meaningful indicators. Perhaps the most meaningful measure of economic progress through the ages, both because of its intrinsic importance and because we have some reliable data, is life expectancy; it increased only slowly from the minimum level at which the species could be sustained rather than go extinct. The most striking aspect of the increase in life expectancy for world populations at various dates over the past 10,000 years is the rapid recent increase in the richer countries since the eighteenth century, and in the poorer countries in the second half of the twentieth country; this is an absolutely unprecedented event, and the most important development in the history of humankind from the standpoint of economics as well as noneconomic welfare.

Some evidence that one might consider as disconfirming the basic proposition of this paper is found in the long-run early history. The total number of human beings who ever lived before, say, 6000 years ago was not small; a reasonable estimate is that of the 77 billion human beings born from 600,000 BC to 1962 AD, 12 billion lived before 6000 BC (with 42 billion from 6000 BC to 1650 AD, and 23 billion from 1650 AD to 1962 AD), to be compared with the more than 5 billion who may be alive now.[1] Of course many of the people born in earlier years died at young ages. But even so, the number of years of human life lived on earth in the long-ago past was not small relative to any recent period. Are these numbers inconsistent with their total intellectual production in light of the thesis of this paper? Later I shall argue that because the production of knowledge depends upon the existing stock of knowledge as well as the population size and density, the slow growth of knowledge in early millennia does not confute the basic thesis.

The tool-using and tool-making revolution kicked off the rapid rise in population around 1,000,000 BC. The aid of various implements gave the food gatherer and hunter access to the widest range of environments. But when the productivity gains from the use of primitive tools had been largely exploited, the rate of population growth fell.

The next rapid jump in population started perhaps 10,000 years ago, when people began to keep herds and cultivate the earth rather than simply foraging for wild plants and game. Once again the rate of population growth abated after the initial productivity gains from the new technology had been exploited, and population size settled down to a near-plateau compared to the rapid growth experienced for a while. The known methods of making a living constituted a constraint to further population growth once the world's population reached a certain size.

These two previous episodes of sharp rise and subsequent fall in the rate of population growth suggest that the present rapid growth—which began perhaps 300 or 350 years ago, in the 1600s—may settle down again when, or if, the gains from the new industrial and agricultural knowledge that followed the "industrial revolution" begin to peter out. And population size may again reach a near-plateau and remain there until another "revolution" due to another major change in technology, society, or psychology. Of course the current knowledge revolution may continue without foreseeable end, and population growth may or may not continue as long as the revolution does. Either way, in this long-term view population size adjusts to productive conditions rather than being an uncontrolled monster.

To return to the many humans who lived in early millennia but produced little new knowledge: If progress were a function of the number of human minds alone, the total medical progress during the long period before, say, 6000 BCE should have been as great as in the last 50 years, during which life expectancy increased rapidly and hugely. But it was not so. Nor was the absence of rapid population growth as a stimulus a reasonable explanation; the presence of sickness and the danger of death certainly have been in all times a sufficiently powerful motivation for major efforts at innovation. So this immediately requires that a theory be more complex than the total number of persons alive among whom the spark of invention and progress might somehow arise spontaneously.

The most reasonable additional explanatory variables are these: (1) Population *density* conduces to the production and transmission of new ideas, according to the theory of Simon Kuznets and the study by Kelley (1972) of Higgs's (1971) data on American inventiveness. (2) Production of new knowledge is influenced by the stock of existing knowledge; the more existing ideas that may be built upon, the greater the propensity to create new ideas. (This is demonstrated for the case of patents in England over many centuries by Simon and Sullivan 1989.)

Evidence from the modern period demonstrating that economic growth in the developed countries has been faster in more recent decades than in more distant decades when population was smaller is found in the work of Maddison, Fellner, and Meguire (the latter finding that the U.S. data do not square with the other countries' data, though it is logically necessary that growth now be faster than, say, 200 years ago (see Simon, forthcoming, for a review of this evidence).

*Cross-sectional evidence.*

Cross-national comparison of the data for recent decades reveals that higher population density is correlated with a higher rate of economic growth (Simon and Gobin 1980).

### *Population Growth and the Growth of Technology*

The next evidence to be presented concerns the bivariate relationships between population and such other variables as knowledge and productivity over the period for which at least some data exists to check for causality.

A long-run measure of the stock of the most important kind of knowledge—agricultural technology—is the number of persons that a single agricultural worker can feed. The complementary variable is the proportion of the labor force that works in agriculture; it was nearly the entire labor force throughout human history. But in about 1600 the proportion began to fall in the richest countries, and it now has reached less than 2 percent in some affluent countries; the decline has unmistakably begun in the poor parts of the world, too. This also is the best long-term measure of the standard of living and of productivity.

A closely related measure of agricultural technology as indicated by agricultural productivity per person is the price in labor time of a given quantity of food. This price has fallen in the U.S. since 1800 by a factor of perhaps 20 (Simon 1992).

A measure of technology related to productivity per person is productivity per unit of land—the amount of land employed to feed an average person. The quantity of land needed to feed a person has declined extraordinarily over the years, in best practice by an astonishing factor of perhaps 25 million, compared with hunting and fishing and by almost as much in standard practice, indicating an extraordinary increase in productivity.

Shifting now to technology in metals production: Analogous to the decline in the price of food as measured by the amount of time required to produce it is the decline in the prices of metals—an enormous fall with respect to the price of labor in rich countries and large even compared with the consumer price index over the past two centuries (Simon 1981; forthcoming), continuing a trend observable for 4,000 years. The supply of copper may be viewed in this context as a final good and a component measure of the standard of living; it may also be seen later as an element in the progress of productivity. The line of causation from population to price seems rather clear here; there is no other reasonable explanation of the increase in supply except an increase in demand and in the supply of minds to produce new ways to increase the supply and invent new substitutes.

The speed and cost of transportation is another good whose technology has measurably improved. (Transport is a good in itself, as well as affecting the supply of food.) In just the past two centuries, speed has risen from the 3-mile-an-hour walking pace of a human or the somewhat faster pace of a horse or ship to hundreds of miles per hour on land and thousands of miles per hour in the air (not even counting space travel).

Long-run data on the increase in the stock of knowledge as measured by the number of scientific journals and patents in the past five centuries, and in human capital as measured by numbers of literate persons and persons with given amounts of education (the absolute numbers are more relevant than the proportions, though the proportion is also of interest), are sufficiently well known as to not need further discussion here.

Some writers have suggested Greece and Rome as counterexamples. But their rates of discoveries of important new ideas were faster in their peak periods of population than before or after those periods (see Simon 1981).

Another long period whose data are relevant is the Dark Ages. Currently most commentators, such as Pirenne, agree that after population declined, the standard of living fell and progress ceased despite the increase in agricultural land per agriculturalist and the consequent drop in the price of land; this might have been caused by the decline in total population or the lack of growth or both. Much the same seems to have been true in the years after the Black Death. In contrast, the rapid increases in population starting around 1000 and 1500 were accompanied by buoyant economic progress.

Simon and Sullivan (1989) show that in England from 1500 to 1800 population and knowledge (as measured by patents) do not just grow together secularly, but there is a causal relationship between them when other variables are held constant.

*Cross-sectional evidence.*

A work tradition beginning with Rostas (1948) shows that when pairs of countries are compared, growth in productivity is higher in those industries in which production is relatively larger; in light of the association between higher production and higher population *ceteris paribus,* this suggests that higher population leads to higher increases in productivity.

Another relevant cross-sectional study is that of Glover and Simon (1975), which shows that road density is greater where population is more dense. And roads are a crucial element in the transmission of knowledge.

## Natural Resources and Population

As North (1981) has written, natural resources have been a major element in discussions of population growth since the first such recorded discussions. The constraint of natural resources must therefore be considered before one can appreciate a theory of human progress in the past despite the perceived limits of natural resources—progress that is without known bounds in the future as natural resource constraints lessen rather than tighten.

Astonishingly, the importance of land and other natural resources diminishes with every passing decade. Such was the great discovery of Schultz about land in 1951, and of Barnett and Morse (1963) about agricultural and mined resources. Their forecasts based on the historical record and theoretical analyses have been borne out perfectly by events since then, as food and all metals, indeed, all natural resources, have continued to get cheaper rather than more expensive.

Natural resources are the most dramatic examples of the fundamental process at work in the long course of economic progress: Increasing population or rising income raises demand for a commodity, which usually implies a higher price. The higher price represents opportunity—for businesses to make a profit and for inventors and institutions to realize their desires to make creative social contributions. Most prospective discoverers fail to find solutions to the problem, and they pay the price themselves. One or more succeed in finding the needed solutions. And usually the outcome, most unexpected though very important, is that the solution leaves humanity better off than before the problem arose. That is, we end up with cheaper resources than before the problem of the rise in price first occurred.

The story of this process at work in the case of energy since about the fifteenth century in England—from wood to coal to oil to nuclear power—is told at length in my 1981 book, as is the story of copper during the 4000 years since Hammurabi.

A formal model of this process using the example of farmland may be found in Simon and Steinman (1991) or in Simon (1992, chapter 5). We simulate the model with meaningful parameters and analyze how the course of food prices and land availability will change over centuries. We also analyze the steady-state properties of the system to show how it is consistent with long-run growth in the standard of living as human numbers increase.

## Very-Long-Run Processes

It should help substantiate the exogeneity of growth to provide evidence on the disaggregated sinews of the process; this is the task of the present section. This section contains the new substantive material conveyed by this article, material which provides the evidence for the propositions that (1) the rate of progress is a function of human numbers; and (2) in the very long run all social and economic dimensions are indeed a function of population size and density and constitute endogenous intermediate variables rather than independent causal variables.

The elements that this section will touch on include the development of markets, social and economic organization, law, disease, and evolved cultural patterns. Here our time horizon is so long that the phenomena that change over such a long period usually are not even mentioned in the context of population economics. These phenomena have been studied little, and because the ground is new the amount of data is small. Hopefully the paucity of data will not mislead the reader about the importance of these phenomena.

### *The Development of Markets*

The size of the market depends upon both the *number of people* and the *level of income*. The number of persons multiplied by their average level of income measures aggregate income, and is perhaps the basic measure of the size of the market. (Of course the sizes of submarkets will be affected by the *distribution* of the total income among persons, but that can be left aside here.) There is a presumption, then, that more people imply bigger markets.

Increased population density also leads to better-organized markets. Hicks (1969) and North (1981) have shown the connection between these variables throughout history at the local and regional level. As noted earlier, this phenomenon was seen vividly after the depopulation of the Black Death. Despite higher wages and increased land availability to cultivators, overall economic conditions apparently were less favorable. There was general economic depression as a result of the disappearance of markets that in turn was caused by lack of people and products to support markets.

A look at mircoeconomic theory with population and market growth in mind immediately suggests many avenues through which there is improved competition when population is larger rather than smaller, especially the effects of having more rather than fewer producers and sellers. In general, a larger number of competitors leads to a more responsive and more rapidly changing marketplace.

Cities, along with infrastructure, seem to have been a crucial precondition of the industrial revolution in England, Holland, and elsewhere. The existence of cities requires relatively dense populations in surrounding areas. Cities and markets are closely related phenomena. Pirenne's magisterial analysis (1925/1969) depends heavily on population growth and size. Larger absolute numbers of people are the basis for increased trade and consequent growth in cities, which in turn strongly influenced the creation of an exchange economy in place of the subsistence economy of the manor.

According to Pirenne, growth in population causing cities to grow also reduced serfdom by offering serfs legal haven in the city, as memorialized in the saying "Town air makes free."

### *Disease*

The evolution of the disease environment is another of the crucial evolutionary processes that population density and growth have influenced. Density of population affects the virulence of disease; sometimes it makes disease spread faster, as in the case of epidemics, and sometimes it suppresses it, as in the case of malaria. And there are further complications: Sometimes increased virulence leads later to immunities that check the spread of diseases. McNeill (1977) describes how the evolution of the disease environment has been greatly influenced in complex ways by population density and therefore by population growth.

For most of the great diseases, the growth of population in earlier centuries represented a one-time "investment" of our species into developing resistance to mass killers; once our ancestors had suffered this experience, later generations could go about their lives with less threats.

A different sequence: By causing the land to be cropped closely, increasing population density reduces the virulence of malaria, the greatest killer of all; an important example was South China, which was only colonized after this process had made it habitable.

A body of knowledge about the prevention and cure of diseases also has evolved, much of it in a prescientific trial-and-error process; an older example is the practice of quarantine. More recently, health knowledge has begun to evolve from systematic scientific work; an example is smallpox vaccination. Such advances in medical practice can be attributed to the combination of a scientific attitude and a greater base of scientific medical knowledge, both of which were enhanced by the industrial revolution; these advances occurred in countries that were experiencing the industrial revolution, and did not occur in countries such as India and China that were outside the ambit of the industrial revolution. This greater capacity to deal actively with the disease environment may be seen as a consequence of population growth.

Events during the industrial revolution are instructive in this regard. The causes of the fall in the death rate are also somewhat unclear, though in recent years scholars have made rapid progress in understanding the phenomenon. Some part of the mortality drop may have been unconnected with economic progress; the climate may have improved and yielded better crops, the rat population may have spontaneously altered its species composition in such fashion that the rigors of plague diminished, and the disease environment may otherwise have become less dangerous. Some part of the improvement may stem from economic progress in only very indirect fashion, if at all, notably through shorter periods of breastfeeding and hence less inhibition of pregnancy. But economic progress was surely responsible for most of the improved life expectancy.

Economic progress, which interactively is the result of population growth, helped people live longer by providing better diets. McKeown (McKeown and Brown 1955; McKeown 1985) has argued forcefully that "the slow growth of the human population before the eighteenth century was due mainly to lack of food, and the rapid increase from that time resulted largely from improved nutrition" (1985, p. 29). Fogel's (1989) work agrees. (The importance of nutrition is surprisingly difficult to establish conclusively, however.)

Economic progress also helped people live longer through development of the physical infrastructure of society, especially provision of purer communal drinking water. Such improvements were not mainly intended to improve health and reduce death, but they nevertheless did so to an important degree. Building such infrastructure requires farming to be sufficiently efficient so that society can afford to employ people on such community projects. Also required is that the population be sufficiently large and dense that such projects are economical. The same is true for roads and other communication systems that contributed to the spread of health technology. (See earlier discussion of road density and population density.)

In some places greater population density must have had short-term negative effects upon health by temporarily lowering the standard of living—the Malthusian "positive check." But in the longer run, the overall result of population growth on the incidence of disease clearly has been positive.

### *Social and Political Organization*

Though it is difficult to pin down statistically, the effect of population size and density upon social and political organization and its role in economic development is given ever greater importance by such scholars as Jones (1981) and McNeill (1963).

Population density and size seem to be related to the mode of organization and the size of the government sector. Stevenson (1968) argues that increasing density leads to better-articulated organization of society; this seems plausible, but the phenomenon is difficult to quantify.

The relationship of population growth to the abolition of feudalism and slavery is controversial and needs further investigation.

It is enlightening to keep in mind a question that is frequently asked: If more people cause there to be more ideas and knowledge, more growth of markets and cities, and hence higher productivity and income, why did not the modernization revolution begin in India and China? This requires more lengthy discussion than this introduction to the subject permits; suffice it to say that it ties into discussion of what Jones calls "the European miracle."

In Europe there seems to have been a nexus of interconnections between loosening of feudal ties, growth of cities, personal economic freedom, political freedom, openness of societies, competition among European states, economic advance, popular government, and population growth. McNeill (1963), Jones (1981) and others have suggested that over several centuries the relative looseness and changeableness of social and economic life in Europe, compared to China and India, helps account for the emergence of modern growth in the West rather than in the East. Change implies economic disequilibria which, as Schultz (1975) reminds us, imply exploitable opportunities leading to augmented effort. (Such disequilibria also cause the production of new knowledge, it would seem.)

### *Evolved Cultural Patterns*

The processes of evolutionary growth extend into technical knowledge, social institutions, language, law, morals, rituals, and practices, all of which affect human productive capacities just as does the evolving stock of land, tools, shelter, and other physical capital—one of the most interesting aspects of this subject. It is plausible that these aspects of human life changed only under the pressure of necessity, as represented by increased population, and then in turn the new conditions influenced the growth of population. If humankind had not developed patterns of behavior and association that increased rather than decreased the amounts of resources available to us, we would not still be here. If, as humankind's numbers increased (or even as numbers remained nearly stationary), behavior had led to diminished supplies of plants and animals, less flint for tools, and disappearing wood for fires and construction, I would not be writing these pages, and you would not be reading them. These processes cannot now be documented for prehistory, of course, but we have begun to develop knowledge about the operation of similar processes in recent decades and the present, e.g., changes in institutions for agricultural research (Hayami and Ruttan 1987).

Evolved cultural patterns include *voluntary exchange among individuals*, and the markets that function to provide resources in increasing quantities, as discussed above; institutions that pass on knowledge, such as schools; libraries, legends and storytellers, all of which store knowledge; and monasteries, laboratories, and research-and-development departments which produce knowledge.

Humankind has evolved into creators and problem solvers to an extent that people's constructive behavior has outweighed their destructive behavior, as evidenced by our increasing life expectancy and richness of consumption. And in recent centuries and decades, this positive net balance has been increasing rather than decreasing. This view of the human as (on balance) a builder conflicts with the view of the human as destroyer, which underlies the thought of many doomsayers.

Paradoxically, *rules and customs that lead to population growth* rather than to population stability or decline may be part of our inherited capacity to deal successfully with resource problems in the long run, though the added people may exacerbate the problems in the short run. Such rules and customs probably lead to long-run success of a society in two ways. First, as noted above, high fertility leads to increased chances of a group's survival, other things being equal. For example, though the Parsis of India have been, as individuals, very successful economically, as a people they seem doomed to the failure of disappearance in the long run due to their marriage and fertility patterns. Second, high fertility leads to resource problems, which then lead to solutions to the problems that usually leave humanity better off in the long run than if the problems had never arisen, in the process discussed earlier. In a more direct chain of events, rules and customs leading to high fertility yield an increased supply of human ingenuity, which responds productively to the increased demand for goods.

Particularly slow to change are *basic institutions of law and convention*. These institutions tend to evolve gradually rather than being altered by political upheaval or legislation. Hayek (1989) argues that property rights and the family are the two most important institutions in determining the economic progress of a nation. He suggests that they, as well as the rest of the rich tapestry of cultural patterns, develop by a process of cultural selection wherein communities that grow in numbers are more likely to have their institutions be dominant in the wider world than are groups that do not increase in population. Much of this evolutionary process has taken place over thousands of years. But the effects were important for economic development; for example, the system of Anglo-Saxon common law and its protection for property surely aided the course of the industrial revolution in England. Therefore, these slow-moving effects of population increase should not be forgotten in our survey of demographic consequences.

Linguistics may be able to cast some light on the rate of change of language to population size. In this respect language may be an important model for change in other subtle elements in culture.

The effect of population density and size upon the refinement and the changes in direction that occur in the law has been hinted at by preliminary studies in the United States relating the size of state to the extent to which decisions are cited. This theme needs to be developed.

Most difficult of all to pin down is the effect of population growth and the industrial revolution, and their proximate effects discussed earlier, upon individual psychology and small-group sociology. Adam

Smith remarks that "the progressive state is in reality the cheerful and the hearty state to all the different orders of the society. The stationary is dull; the declining melancholy." And it was a commonplace during the earlier part of the industrial revolution that industrial work discipline, including attention to the daily time schedule for work hours, was both important and slow to develop. Many writers have discussed the mentality of progress and the notion of systematic scientific progress; both ideas were concomitants of the industrial revolution. However accurate these observations about psychological and small-group effects may be, however, they do not stand on the same level of demonstrated fact as do the phenomena discussed in the earlier parts of this paper. Yet the brevity of this treatment should not be taken as suggesting that these factors may not be of great significance. (On the other hand, perhaps human nature should be seen as having been changed relatively little by the industrial revolution. The meaning of "little" and "much" are quite subjective, of course.)

## Summary and Conclusions

This paper outlines a theory of the role of "human capital" that fits the very-long-run trends. It discusses some of the elements that affect the *speed of adjustment* to population change, conditions which are different at different times in history and vary from place to place.

1. The state of knowledge clearly is the dominant element that varies in the long run. It is affected by population growth and density, as knowledge in turn affects population growth and density.

2. Interrelated with changes in knowledge and production technique are changes in the structure of society. These structural changes also are influenced by population variables, and vice versa. There is increasing recognition of the importance of social and economic structure in economic development in even the short run. And population affects these forces in the long run.

3. The growth of markets, with their many associated phenomena, has been a function of population size and density. More people mean both more buyers and more sellers, and hence less monopoly and more competition and competitive effort.

4. Slowest-changing are the habits, rituals, language, law, morals, and all manner of social institutions, including sexual and childraising practices. All of these elements are subject to processes of evolutionary change. They not only are affected by population variables, but in turn influence population growth and—differentially—the likelihoods of survival of different human groups. Also disease affects in both directions. Here we have moved all the way to full biology-like evolutionary thinking, which is at the other end of the methodological spectrum from the sort of physics-like thinking that we apply in very-short-run analysis when the relevant elements are known and fixed. But the evolutionary processes in question are social and cultural rather than biological.

## NOTE

1. A more recent estimate is 3.8 billion before 40,000 BCE, 39 billion from 40,000 BCE to the start of the Common Era, and 22.6 billion from the year 1 up until the year 1750, plus another 10.4 billion from then until 1950, and 4.3 billion from then until 1987, for a total of perhaps 80.3 billion (Bourgeois-Pichat 1989, p. 90). The fact that, although Bourgeois-Pichat did not make reference to Desmond (1975), the two estimates are so close to each other lends confidence to them.

## References

Barnett, Harold, and Chandler Morse. 1963. *Scarcity and Growth.* Baltimore: Johns Hopkins University Press.

Boserup, Ester. 1965. *The Conditions of Economic Growth.* London: Allen and Unwin.

Bourgeois-Pichat, J. 1989. "From the 20th to the 21st Century: Europe and Its Population After the Year 2000," *Population,* English Selection 1 (September): 57–90.

Clark, Colin. 1957. *The Conditions of Economic Progress,* 2nd edition. New York: Macmillan.

Clough, Shepard B. 1951, 1957. *The Rise and Fall of Civilization.* New York: Columbia University Press.

Deevey, Edward S. 1960. "The Human Population," *Scientific American* 203: 195–204. Reprinted in *Man and the Ecosphere,* Paul R. Ehrlich, John P. Holdren, and Richard W. Holm, eds. San Francisco: W.H. Freeman, 1971.

Desmond, Annabelle. 1975. "How Many People Have Ever Lived on Earth?" *Population Bulletin* 18: 1–9. Reprinted in *Population Studies,* 2nd edition, Kenneth C.W. Kammeyer, ed. Chicago: Rand McNally, 1975.

Fogel, Robert William. 1989. "Secular Trends in Mortality, Nutritional Status, and Labor Productivity." Mimeo, February 2.

Fredericksen, Peter C. 1981. "Further Evidence on the Relationship Between Population Density and Infrastructure: The Philippines and Electrification," *Economic Development and Cultural Change* 29: 749–58.

Gimpel, Jean. 1977. *The Medieval Machine.* New York: Penguin.

Glover, Donald, and Julian L. Simon. 1975. "The Effect of Population Density Upon Infrastructure: The Case of Roadbuilding," *Economic Development and Cultural Change* 23, 3 (April).

Hayami, Yujiro, and Vernon W. Ruttan. 1987. "Population Growth and Agricultural Productivity." In *Population Growth and Economic Development: Issues and Evidence,* D. Gale Johnson and Ronald D. Lee, eds. Madison, WI: University of Wisconsin Press, pp. 57–104.

Hayek, Friedrich A. 1960. *The Constitution of Liberty.* Chicago: University of Chicago Press.

_____. 1989. *The Fatal Conceit.* Chicago: University of Chicago Press.

Hicks, Sir John. 1969. *A Theory of Economic History.* London: Oxford University Press.

Higgs, Robert. 1971. "American Inventiveness, 1870–1920," *Journal of Political Economy* 79: 661–667.

Jones, Eric L. 1981. *The European Miracle.* New York: Cambridge University Press.

_____. 1988. *Growth Recurring.* New York: Oxford University Press.

Kelley, Allen. 1972. "Scale Economies, Inventive Activity, and the Economics of American Population Growth," *Explorations in Economic History* (Fall): 35–72.

_____. 1976. "Demographic Change and the Size of the Government Sector," *Southern Economic Journal* 43, 2 (October).

Klein, Herbert Arthur. 1974. *The Science of Measurement: A Historical Survey.* New York: Dover Publications.

Lal, Deepak. 1990. *Cultural Stability and Economic Stagnation: India, 1500 BC–1980 AD.* London and New York: Oxford University Press.

Leakey, Richard E. 1981. *The Making of Mankind.* New York: Dutton.

McKeown, Thomas. 1985. "Food, Infection, and Population." In *Hunger and History,* Rotberg and Rabb, eds. London: Cambridge University Press, pp. 29–50.

McKeown, Thomas, and R.G. Brown. 1955. "Medical Evidence Related to English Population Changes in the Eighteenth Century," *Population Studies* 9: 119–141.

McNeill, William H. 1963. *The Rise of the West—A History of the Human Community.* Chicago: University of Chicago Press.

_____. 1977. *Plagues and Peoples.* Garden City, NY: Anchor Books.

North, Douglass C. 1981. *Structure and Change in Economic History.* New York: Norton.

Pirenne, Henri. 1925/1969. *Medieval Cities.* Princeton: Princeton University Press.

Rostas, Leo. 1948. "Comparative Productivity in British and American Industry." NBER Occasional Paper 13.

Schultz, Theodore W. 1951. "The Declining Economic Importance of Land," *Economic Journal* 61 (December): 725–740.

_____. 1975. "The Value of the Ability to Deal with Disequilibria," *Journal of Economic Literature* 13, 3: 827–46.

Simon, Julian L. 1977. *The Economics of Population Growth.* Princeton: Princeton University Press.

_____. 1978. "An Integration of the Invention-Pull and Population-Push Theories of Economic-Demographic History." In *Research in Population Economics,* Vol. I, Julian L. Simon, ed. Greenwich: JAI Press.

_____. 1981. *The Ultimate Resource.* Princeton: Princeton University Press.

_____. 1992. *Population and Development in Poor Countries.* Princeton: Princeton University Press.

_____, ed. Forthcoming. *The State of Humanity.* Boston: Basil Blackwell.

Simon, Julian L., and Roy Gobin. 1980. "The Relationship Between Population and Economic Growth in LDC's." In *Research in Population Economics,* Vol. II, Julian Simon and Julie Da Vanzo, eds. Greenwich: JAI Press.

Simon, Julian L., and Richard J. Sullivan. 1989. "Population Size, Knowledge Stock, and Other Determinants of Agricultural Publication and Patenting: England, 1541–1850," *Explorations in Economic History* 26: 21–44.

Simon, Julian L., and Gunter Steinman. 1981. "Population Growth and Phelps' Technical Progress Model." In *Research in Population Economics,* Vol III, J. Simon and P. Lindert, eds. Greenwich: JAI Press, 239–54.

_____. 1991. "Population Growth, Farmland, and the Long-Run Standard of Living," *Journal of Population Economics* 4, 1: 37–51.

Steinman, Gunter, and Julian L. Simon. 1981. "Phelps' Technical Progress Model Generalized," *Economic Letters* 5: 177–82.

Stevenson, Robert F. 1968. *Population and Political Systems in Tropical Africa.* New York: Columbia University Press.

Tinsley, Brian A. 1980. "Technical Development and Colonization as Factors in the Long-Term Variation in Limits to Growth," *Cosmic Search,* Year End.

# INDEX

# About the Institute

The W.E. Upjohn Institute for Employment Research is a nonprofit research organization devoted to finding and promoting solutions to employment-related problems at the national, state, and local level. It is an activity of the W.E. Upjohn Unemployment Trustee Corporation, which was established in 1932 to administer a fund set aside by the late Dr. W.E. Upjohn, founder of The Upjohn Company, to seek ways to counteract the loss of employment income during economic downturns.

The Institute is funded largely by income from the W.E. Upjohn Unemployment Trust, supplemented by outside grants, contracts, and sales of publications. Activities of the Institute are comprised of the following elements: (1) a research program conducted by a resident staff of professional social scientists; (2) a competitive grant program, which expands and complements the internal research program by providing financial support to researchers outside the Institute; (3) a publications program, which provides the major vehicle for the dissemination of research by staff and grantees, as well as other selected work in the field; and (4) an Employment Management Services division, which manages most of the publicly funded employment and training programs in the local area.

The broad objectives of the Institute's research, grant, and publication programs are to: (1) promote scholarship and experimentation on issues of public and private employment and unemployment policy; and (2) make knowledge and scholarship relevant and useful to policymakers in their pursuit of solutions to employment and unemployment problems.

Current areas of concentration for these programs include: causes, consequences, and measures to alleviate unemployment; social insurance and income maintenance programs; compensation; workforce quality; work arrangements; family labor issues; labor-management relations; and regional economic development and local labor markets.